Figuring Out Society

An introduction to the use of quantitative methods in the social sciences

Ronald L. Meek

Fontana/Collins

First published in Fontana 1972
Second impression September 1974

Copyright © Ronald L. Meek 1972

Printed in Great Britain for the
Publishers Wm Collins Sons & Co Ltd
14 St James's Place, London SW1
By Richard Clay (The Chaucer Press), Ltd
Bungay, Suffolk

Contents

Preface

'Then it will be fitting, Glaucon, . . . to persuade those who are to share in the highest affairs of the city to take to calculation, and embrace it in no amateur spirit'
(*Plato*, The Republic, *Book VII*).

The young men who were to become the guardians of the City Beautiful, Plato proclaimed, must first and foremost study calculation and geometry. These things, he said, were used by all crafts, all modes of thought, and all sciences. They were an essential part of the art of war, but they also drew men's souls towards truth. For the guardians, who had to be both warriors and philosophers, they were therefore the basis of all effective action and understanding.

In the last twenty or thirty years, as the result of one of the most remarkable intellectual revolutions of the century, we have suddenly come much closer to the realisation of Plato's dream. 'Calculation', which was formerly used more or less exclusively in the physical sciences, is now coming to be used very extensively in the social and behavioural sciences as well. The application of quantitative methods in these new spheres has opened up a vast and fascinating field of inquiry, in which important discoveries are being made about men's behaviour and relations with one another in society.

In one respect, it is true, Plato would probably have disapproved of some of these new developments. He was very much against 'calculation' being used for commercial ends rather than for the sake of knowledge; and it is undeniable that a number of the new quantitative techniques—particularly those which usually go under the blanket title of 'Operations Research'—are being applied and developed by industrial firms, with a view to increasing their economic efficiency, and therefore their profits.

But economic efficiency is the concern of public enterprises as well as private ones, and it is also the concern of the central government in its capacity as the supreme manager or overseer of the country's economic life as a whole. And it is not only economics which is being revolutionised by the new techniques, but the other social sciences too. The use of the theory of games and related techniques as tools of research in psychology, anthropology, politics, and military strategy; the increasing use of mathematical and statistical methods in economic history; the development of new techniques of measurement and mathematical models in the broad field of sociology; the use of cost-benefit analysis in town planning and in the management of expenditure on education and public health—all these are indications of a profound change which is taking place today in the general orientation and methodology of the social sciences as a whole.

What we are witnessing, in essence, is the rise of a new science of decision-making in the general field of social and economic relations—a science of 'social engineering', if you like, the purpose of which is to help human beings, living as they do in complex and uncertain societies, to make *rational choices* between the various alternatives which confront them.

The future 'guardians' of our society, then, if they are to be equal to the challenges of the age we are now entering, must 'take to calculation, and embrace it in no amateur spirit'. And it is here that the difficulty arises. While the trend in the social sciences towards the use of quantitative methods is rapidly increasing, the number of students entering the social science departments at our universities without a good grounding in mathematics remains very considerable. Many young people, who are keenly and quite properly interested in getting to grips with the burning social problems which confront us, abandon mathematics at O-level, on the mistaken assumption that social science subjects, like arts subjects, do not require numeracy. The result is that so far from 'taking to calculation' in the manner that Plato recommended, they often display a dislike and fear of it which are very difficult to overcome, and which all too often lead to disillusionment and a cynical rejection of the new techniques.

The present book, written by a mathematical simpleton for mathematical simpletons, is meant as a modest contribution to the solution of this problem. It is addressed mainly to sixth-formers, first-year university students, and interested members of the general public who are concerned about social problems but who are puzzled and repelled by the new quantitative methods which social scientists are increasingly using to tackle them. It assumes no previous mathematical knowledge other than that of the most elementary kind, and it does not make any very substantial advances on the mathematical front as it goes along. Its aim is simply to open a door and give the reader a glimpse of the exciting new world which lies on the other side: it does not set out to take him on a conducted tour of that world. I hope, however, that the reader, having discovered that the journey is not as arduous as he might have expected, will make further explorations of the territory himself.

For permission to reproduce tables and passages of text, to redraw diagrams, and to summarise the main argument of works in copyright, thanks are due to: The University of Chicago Press for a diagram and summary of material from 'An Illustration of the Use of Analytical Theory in Sociology . . .' by E. V. Schneider and S. Krupp, in *The American Journal of Sociology* (May 1965); Messrs Chapman and Hall Ltd, and Dr. John R. Meyer for quotations, tables, and a summary of material from 'The Economics of Slavery in the Antebellum South' in *Studies in Econometric History*, by Alfred H. Conrad and John R. Meyer; and the Aldine Publishing Company and Dr. Meyer for the same material from Alfred H. Conrad and John R. Meyer, *The Economics of Slavery: And Other Studies in Econometric History* (Chicago: Aldine Publishing Company, 1964), copyright © 1964 by Alfred H. Conrad and John R. Meyer; The McGraw-Hill Book Company for a quotation from *Operations Research and Quantitative Economics*, by H. Thiel, J. C. G. Boot, and T. Kloek; the editor, *The Manchester School* for a diagram and summary of material from 'Estimate of the Rate of Return to Education in Great Britain', by D. Henderson-Stewart (September 1965); the editor, *Journal of the Operations Research Society of America* for diagrams and a summary of material from 'Military Decision and Game Theory', by O. G. Haywood (November 1954); the University of Pittsburgh Press for a quotation from 'The Game of Chicken', by A. Rapoport and A. M. Chammah in *Game Theory and the Behavioral Sciences*, edited I. R. Buchler and H. G. Nutini; the editor, *Population Studies*, and the author for diagrams and a summary of material from 'Theory of Population and Modern Economic Analysis', by A. T. Peacock (November, 1962); John Wiley and Sons for material from *Decision*

Making Through Operations Research, by R. J. Thierauf and
R. A. Grosse; the editor, Yale University Publications in
Anthropology for a summary of material from 'Jamaican
Fishing: A Game Theory Analysis', by William Davenport
(no. 59, 1960).

I am greatly indebted to Mr. Michael Turnbull, of Fontana
Paperbacks, who has given me invaluable advice on matters
of presentation; and to Mr. Howard Rees, of the Department
of Economics at Leicester University, who has gone over my
mathematics with a tooth-comb. If any crudities of expression
or illegitimate mathematical short cuts remain, they are my
fault and not theirs.

R. L. M.

Chapter 1
A drop too much

In which we meet the late Mr. James Berry—public hangman, econometrician, and forgotten genius—who introduces us to the concept of the functional interdependence of variables.

In 1884, when the post of Public Executioner of Great Britain fell vacant, the person appointed—out of a very large number of applicants—was Mr. James Berry.[1]

The choice was a sound one. Mr. Berry was a handsome man, the beauty of his features being marred only by a long, deep scar extending down his right cheek and another great scar across his forehead.[2] He was a man of aesthetic sensibility, as one can see from the visiting card reproduced overleaf, which he had printed early in his professional career. 'The wording was in black', Mr. Berry tells us, 'with the fern in green, and the border in gold.'[3]

He was also, in his own way, something of a social scientist. He was a technological innovator, being the first British hangman to use the brass eyelet.[4] He was an economist: in his autobiography there is a chapter headed 'Hanging: From a Business Point of View', in which he makes an earnest plea for the substitution of time rates for piece rates.[5]

Above all, he was a pioneer in the application of quantitative methods to the science of which he was a practitioner. His search for a solution to a grave professional problem led him by a process of trial and error—many trials, and I am afraid one or two errors—to a number of interesting quantitative discoveries, a discussion of which will afford a highly

1. The information which follows about Mr. Berry's life and work is taken largely from his autobiography, *My Experiences as an Executioner*, edited by H. Snowden Ward, which was originally published in 1892. This remarkable work, having been out of print for many years, was reprinted by David & Charles in 1972, with a new introduction and additional appendices by Jonathan Goodman.
2. *My Experiences as an Executioner*, p. 13.
3. *Ibid.*, p. 134.
4. *Ibid.*, p. 39.
5. *Ibid.*, pp. 117–123.

instructive introduction to our study of the use of quantitative methods in the social sciences.

Mr. Berry's problem—which arose, oddly enough, out of his extreme tender-heartedness[6]—was simply this: to select a drop of a length which would cause instantaneous death by dislocation of the neck. It was rather important that the drop should be neither too short nor too long. If it were too short, the client would die by slow strangulation. If it were too long, there was a danger that his head would be pulled right off.

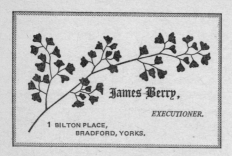

James Berry,

EXECUTIONER.

1 BILTON PLACE,
BRADFORD, YORKS.

The solution to Mr. Berry's problem would have been fairly easy if all murderers were the same weight, but in fact, as he soon found out, they vary greatly. Clearly the length of drop which would avoid the two unpleasant consequences just noted would depend upon the weight of the client. The heavier the man, other things being equal, the shorter the optimum length of drop. But *how*, precisely, were these two crucial quantities—weight of client and optimum length of drop—related to one another? Was it possible to make some general quantitative statement about their relationship, of such a kind that it could be used as the basis for a kind of Ready Reckoner for Hangmen? What Mr. Berry needed, in effect, was some kind of table, graph, or arithmetical formula which would enable him, once he knew the weight of his client, to work out immediately the optimum length of drop required for him.[7]

Mr. Berry began to experiment. His first commission, as he

6. *My Experiences as an Executioner*, p. 12.
7. In the modern jargon, we would say that Mr. Berry's problem was to find the form of the *functional relationship* between an *independent variable* (weight of client) and a *dependent variable* (optimum length of drop). These terms will be more fully elucidated in Chapter 2.

tells us, 'was to execute Robert Vickers and William Innes, two miners who were condemned to death for the murder of two game-keepers. The respective weights were 10 stone 4 lb. and 9 stone 6 lb., and I gave them drops of 8 ft. 6 in. and 10 ft. respectively. In both cases death was instantaneous, and the prison surgeon gave me a testimonial that the execution was satisfactory in every respect.' [8]

Let us record these two successes of Mr. Berry's on a graph (Figure 1.1), where the client's weight (in stones) is measured along the horizontal axis, and the length of the drop (in feet) is measured up the vertical axis. [9] Vickers was 10 stone 4 lb. and was given a drop of 8 ft. 6 in., so let us put a dot labelled Vickers at the point on the graph which is directly above 10 stone 4 lb. on the horizontal axis and level with 8 ft. 6 in. on the vertical axis. Innes was 9 stone 6 lb. and was given a drop of 10 ft., so let us put a dot labelled Innes at the point on the graph which is directly above 9 stone 6 lb. on the horizontal axis and level with 10 ft. on the vertical axis. We shall use this graph several times as our story proceeds, in order to illustrate the progress of Mr. Berry's investigations.

With the prison surgeon's testimonial on his mantelpiece, Mr. Berry could now put his feet up and do a bit of thinking. What he wanted, as we have seen, was some kind of table, graph, or arithmetical formula from which, given the weight of his client, he could readily calculate the appropriate length of drop. But as yet he did not have nearly enough concrete data upon which to base a Ready Reckoner of this kind. All he knew was that a drop of 8 ft. 6 in. worked satisfactorily with a man of 10 stone 4 lb., and a drop of 10 ft. with a man of 9 stone 6 lb. But suppose the man's weight were 8 stone, or 12 stone? What would the appropriate length of the drop be then? Mr. Berry realised that he would not be able to give a *certain* answer to such questions until he had done a lot more experimenting.

But obviously he had to start with *some* hypothesis, however rough and provisional, about the correct relationship between weight and drop. The difficulty here was that he had only two observations to go on; and he seems to have realised instinctively that this was not enough. So, like all good scientists

8. *My Experiences as an Executioner*, p. 31.
9. The principles according to which graphs are constructed are set out in the Mathematical Appendix, Section 9, pp. 213–16.

with limited concrete data at their disposal, he fell back on intuition to provide himself with a third 'observation' which would act as a kind of basis. Relying on some sort of sixth sense, he *assumed* that a man of 14 stone would require a drop of 8 ft., thereby providing himself with a third point of reference to add to the other two.

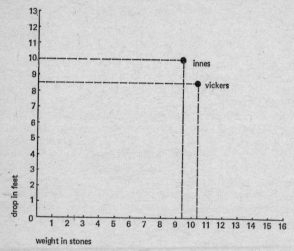

Figure 1·1

His task now was to derive from this still rather meagre set of observations the best possible working hypothesis about the true underlying relationship between weight and drop. 'Taking a man of 14 stones as a basis', he tells us, 'and giving him a drop of 8 ft., which is what I thought necessary, I calculated that every half-stone lighter weight would require a two inches longer drop.'[10] This hypothesis he embodied in a table,[11] which he entered as follows in his books:

10. *My Experiences as an Executioner*, p. 31.
11. The way in which a statistician would describe what Mr. Berry was in effect doing when he constructed his table would be to say that he was trying to fit a *regression line* to his three observations. In other words, he was trying to find the straight line which in some sense 'fitted' the 'Vickers', 'Innes', and 'Basis' dots better than any other. This theme will be taken up again in Chapter 3.

Weight in Stones	Length of Drop	Weight in Stones	Length of Drop
14	8 ft. 0 in.	10½	9 ft. 2 in.
13½	8 ft. 2 in.	10	9 ft. 4 in.
13	8 ft. 4 in.	9½	9 ft. 6 in.
12½	8 ft. 6 in.	9	9 ft. 8 in.
12	8 ft. 8 in.	8½	9 ft. 10 in.
11½	8 ft. 10 in.	8	10 ft. 0 in.
11	9 ft. 0 in.		

Mr. Berry's table, as the reader will see, stopped at 8 stone—presumably because he did not anticipate having to execute a murderer any lighter than that. But Mr. Berry's hypothesis in itself, as he actually stated it, did not mention anything about 8 stone. All it said was that a man of 14 stone would require a drop of 8 ft., and that 'every half-stone lighter weight would require a two inches longer drop.' If this statement were true, it would follow that a man of 7½ stone would require a drop of 10 ft. 2 in.; a man of 7 stone a drop of 10 ft. 4 in.; and so on. For every half-stone by which the weight went down, the optimum length of drop would go up by 2 in. So we could complete Mr. Berry's table, taking it right to the logical extreme of a weight of zero, as follows:

Weight in Stones	Length of Drop	Weight in Stones	Length of Drop
7½	10 ft. 2 in.	3½	11 ft. 6 in.
7	10 ft. 4 in.	3	11 ft. 8 in.
6½	10 ft. 6 in.	2½	11 ft. 10 in.
6	10 ft. 8 in.	2	12 ft. 0 in.
5½	10 ft. 10 in.	1½	12 ft. 2 in.
5	11 ft. 0 in.	1	12 ft. 4 in.
4½	11 ft. 2 in.	½	12 ft. 6 in.
4	11 ft. 4 in.	0	12 ft. 8 in.

Let us now plot each of these 29 combinations of weight and drop on our graph, and see what they look like (Figure 1.2). The dots go up in a straight line from right to left, starting at the one labelled 'Basis' (which represents a weight of 14 stone and a drop of 8 ft.), going up gently more or less midway

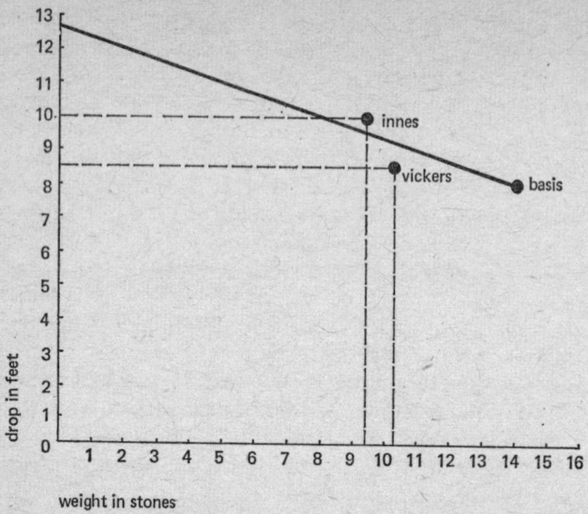

Figure 1·2

between Innes and Vickers, and finishing at a point 12⅔ ft. up the vertical axis. To get from one dot to the next we always move a given distance representing a half-stone horizontally to the left, and then a given distance representing 2 in. (or $\frac{1}{6}$ of a foot) vertically upwards. Since these distances do not alter as we proceed from dot to dot, the dots as a whole necessarily lie in a straight line—i.e., in a line whose *slope* remains the same throughout.[12] In fact, since the dots so obviously form a straight line and are so close together, we might as well join them up. We will then have a line from which we can read off the appropriate length of drop for a man of *any* weight, and not merely for men of the 29 specific weights represented by the dots.[13]

Mr. Berry embodied his hypothesis in a table; we have gone

12. We measure the slope of a line in much the same way as we measure the slope of a hill. (See Mathematical Appendix, section 10, pp. 216–19.) In the case we are considering, for every $\frac{1}{2}$ stone we move horizontally to the left we move $\frac{1}{6}$ of a foot vertically upwards. The slope of the line is therefore $\frac{1}{6}$: $\frac{1}{2}$, i.e. 1 in 3, or $\frac{1}{3}$.

13. The assumption we make when we join up the dots is that if a man of, say, 11 stone requires a drop of 9 ft. 0 in., and a man of 10½ stone requires a drop of 9 ft. 2 in., then a man whose weight is half way between 11 and 10½ stone will require a drop half way between 9 ft. 0 in. and 9 ft. 2 in.—and so on for all other intermediate points.

further and embodied it in a line on a graph. It will be very useful to us later if we now go a little further still and embody it in an arithmetical formula. The line on the graph will help us here. Let us imagine ourselves starting at the point at the top of the line, which represents a weight in stones of zero and a drop in feet of $12\frac{2}{3}$, and gradually going down the line, observing what is happening to weight and drop as we do so.

For every stone by which the weight rises above zero, the length of drop falls below $12\frac{2}{3}$ ft. by 4 in., i.e. by $\frac{1}{3}$ of a foot. So we can say immediately that the appropriate length of the drop will always be $12\frac{2}{3}$ ft. *minus* $\frac{1}{3}$ of a foot for every stone the client weighs. Since this is rather a mouthful, let us express it in a kind of shorthand, using the letter 'D' to mean 'length of Drop in feet' and the letter 'W' to mean 'Weight of client in stones'. In this shorthand our formula then becomes [14]

$$D = 12\frac{2}{3} - \frac{1}{3}W$$

Let us check that this formula gives us the same result as both the table and the graph. What is the appropriate drop for a man of, say, 8 stone? According to the table it is 10 ft. 0 in. We get the same result if we use the line on the graph as our Ready Reckoner: the drop corresponding to the point on the line immediately above 8 stone is 10 ft. 0 in. And if we use the formula, substituting 8 for W, we get

$$\begin{aligned} D &= 12\tfrac{2}{3} - \tfrac{1}{3} . 8 \\ &= 12\tfrac{2}{3} - 2\tfrac{2}{3} \\ &= 10 \end{aligned}$$

Like all good scientists, Mr. Berry now set about *testing* this hypothesis concerning the relationship between weight and length of drop. In other words, he hanged people according to his table and watched what happened. I am pleased to be able to record, however, that Mr. Berry was no dogmatist: he was always ready to modify his procedure if he felt that the circumstances required it. For instance, he tells us, 'in the case of persons of very fleshy build, who often have weak bones and muscles about the neck, I have reduced the drop by a quarter or half of the distance indicated by the table . . .'[15]

Until 30th November, 1885, everything went, as one might say, without a hitch. On that day Mr. Berry was faced with a

14. Note that the first figure on the right of the $=$ sign, $12\frac{2}{3}$, represents the point at which the line hits the vertical axis, and that the second figure, $\frac{1}{3}$, represents the *slope* of the line (see footnote 12 on p. 18).

15. *My Experiences as an Executioner*, p. 32.

really thorny problem, in the shape of a murderer named Robert Goodale, who weighed 15 stone. The graph shows the trouble: the line starts with 'Basis' at 14 stone, and contains no information whatever which is relevant to a client of any greater weight than this.

Well, a common procedure in such cases is to *extrapolate*— i.e., to extend the line, and this is what Mr. Berry in effect did. If every half-stone *lighter* weight (than 14 stone) would require a two inches *longer* drop (than 8 ft.), then it seemed reasonable to assume that every half-stone *heavier* weight (than 14 stone) would require a two inches *shorter* drop (than 8 ft.). Goodale was 15 stone, reasoned Mr. Berry, so the drop ought to be 7 ft. 8 in. Taking this length as his starting-point, he decided to reduce it to 5 ft. 9 in. because the muscles of Goodale's neck 'did not appear well developed and strong'. Even this, however, was not short enough, as Mr. Berry himself explains in a melancholy passage in his autobiography. One would like to draw a veil over what actually happened, but in the interests of science we must face the harsh reality: the jerk severed the murderer's head entirely from the body, so that both fell together to the bottom of the pit. 'Death was instantaneous', wrote the tender-hearted Mr. Berry, 'so that the poor fellow had not suffered in any way; but it was terrible to think that such a revolting thing should have occurred . . . The inquest was a trying ordeal for all concerned.'[16]

From the point of view of Mr. Berry's scientific quest, however, the important thing was that the relationship between weight and drop postulated in his initial hypothesis had been proved to be wrong—and something had to be done about it. His genius was equal to the occasion. He rejected his first hypothesis and formulated another. The relationship between weight and drop, he now said, should be such that the client's fall finished with a striking force of 24 cwt.

If this was the proper relationship, then, how could one go about finding, for a client of any given weight, what the appropriate length of drop actually was? To do this, the ingenious Mr. Berry began by consulting textbooks on physics, and compiled a table showing the striking force of *falling bodies* of various weights falling through different distances. This table, which he proudly publishes in his autobiography, is reproduced on page 21.

16. *My Experiences as an Executioner*, p. 64.

Scale Showing the Striking Force of Falling Bodies at Different Distances

Distance Falling in Feet Zero	8 Stone			9 Stone			10 Stone			11 Stone			12 Stone			13 Stone			14 Stone			15 Stone		
	Cwt.	Qr.	lb.	Cwt.	Qr.	lb.	Cwt.	Qr.	lb.	Cwt.	Qr.	lb.	Cwt.	Qr.	lb.	Cwt.	Qr.	lb.	Cwt.	Qr.	lb.	Cwt.	Qr.	lb.
1 ft.	8	0	0	9	0	0	10	0	0	11	0	0	12	0	0	13	0	0	14	0	0	15	0	0
2 ,,	11	1	15	12	2	23	14	0	14	15	2	4	16	3	22	18	1	12	19	3	2	21	0	21
3 ,,	13	3	16	15	2	15	17	1	14	19	0	12	20	3	11	22	2	9	24	1	8	26	0	7
4 ,,	16	0	0	18	0	0	20	0	0	22	0	0	24	0	0	26	0	0	28	0	0	30	0	0
5 ,,	17	2	11	19	3	5	22	0	0	24	0	22	26	1	16	28	2	11	30	3	5	33	0	0
6 ,,	19	2	11	22	0	5	24	2	0	26	3	22	29	1	16	31	2	11	34	1	5	36	3	0
7 ,,	21	0	22	23	3	11	26	2	0	29	0	16	31	3	5	34	1	22	37	0	11	39	3	0
8 ,,	22	2	22	25	2	4	28	1	14	31	0	23	34	0	5	36	3	15	39	2	25	42	2	7
9 ,,	24	0	11	27	0	12	30	0	14	33	0	23	36	0	16	39	0	18	42	0	19	45	0	21
10 ,,	25	1	5	28	1	23	31	2	14	34	3	4	37	3	22	41	0	12	44	1	2	47	1	21

To use this new Ready Reckoner, we first find the weight of the client in stones. We then look down the appropriate column of weights until we come to the figure nearest to 24 cwt. The figure level with this in the left-hand column will then indicate the appropriate length of drop.

Suppose, for example, that the murderer weighs 10 stone. We want a length of drop for him which will ensure that he finishes his fall with a striking force of 24 cwt. We cast our eye down the column of weights headed '10 Stone' until we come to the figure nearest to 24 cwt. This is clearly 24 cwt. 2 qr. 0 lb. The figure level with this in the left-hand column is 6 ft. So if we give our man a drop of 6 ft. or thereabouts, he will finish his fall with a striking force of about 24 cwt., and according to Mr. Berry's second hypothesis that will do the trick nicely.

Can we find an arithmetical formula which embodies the new relationship between weight and drop implicit in Mr. Berry's second hypothesis? We may be able to find a clue if we look carefully at the 'falling bodies' table. Have a look at the weights (in cwt.) along the row which is level with *4 ft.* in the left-hand column. Each of them is *twice* the weight (in stones) at the head of the relevant column. Now have a look at the weights (in cwt.) along the row which is level with *9 ft.* in the left-hand column. Each of them is approximately *three times* the weight (in stones) at the head of the relevant column.

Is there any common relationship between the length and the multiple in these two cases? Yes, there is—2 is the *square root* of 4, and 3 is the *square root* of 9. This fact suggests that there may be a quantitative relationship between striking force in cwt., weight of falling body in stones, and length of drop in feet, of the following kind:

Striking force (in cwt.) = weight (in stones) multiplied by square root of drop (in feet)

When we do the sums, we find that this relationship does in fact hold in *all* the cases, and not merely in the two we have considered—not always absolutely accurately, it is true, but near enough for all practical purposes.

Now according to Mr. Berry's new hypothesis the striking force must always be 24 cwt., if the drop is to be of the optimum length. It follows from this, and from the formula in the last paragraph, that for any given weight in stones (W) of the client, the length of the drop in feet (D) must be such that

24 (the necessary striking force) $= W . \sqrt{D}$

That is (turning the equation round),

$$\sqrt{D} = \frac{24}{W}$$

That is (squaring everything on both sides),

$$D = \frac{576}{W^2}$$

Once again we have provided ourselves with a very convenient Ready Reckoner in formula form. If we know the weight of the client, we can immediately work out the appropriate length of drop. For a man of 8 stone, for example,

$$D = \frac{576}{8^2} = \frac{576}{64} = 9 \text{ ft.}$$

We can graph this relationship by taking various different values for W, working out what the value of D will be for each of these, plotting the dots on the graph, and joining them up. When we do, it comes out as the curve in Figure 1.3.

We now see before our eyes a plausible explanation of the Goodale tragedy. The true relationship between weight and drop, perhaps, is not the straight-line one represented by the formula $D = 12\frac{2}{3} - \frac{1}{3}W$, but the curvilinear one represented by the formula $D = \frac{576}{W^2}$. If this is true, then Mr. Berry's first hypothesis over-estimated the length of drop to be given to murderers whose weight was more than about $7\frac{1}{2}$ stone, and the greater the weight of the murderer the greater was this degree of over-estimation. Goodale, whose weight was 15 stone, ought in fact to have been given a drop of something under 3 ft.

Mr. Berry now began working in accordance with his new hypothesis, and there were no more unhappy incidents until another red-letter day—20th August, 1891—when a further mishap somewhat similar to the previous one occurred. But the circumstances on this occasion were very different: by an odd quirk of fate the mishap did not disprove, but brilliantly confirmed, Mr. Berry's new hypothesis.

On the date in question Mr. Berry was due to execute one John Conway at Kirkdale Gaol, Liverpool. Conway's weight was just over 11 stone, and Mr. Berry decided, after seeing him, that the length of drop should be 4 ft. 6 in., a little below the scale rate. The prison doctor, however, Barr by name, told Mr. Berry that he was to give a drop of 6 ft. 9 in. Mr. Berry,

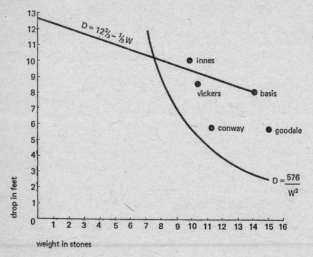

Figure 1·3

rightly indignant at this interference with his autonomy, and suspecting that Dr. Barr was acting 'under authority', told him that a drop of this length would pull the man's head off altogether, and finally refused to go on with the execution unless some modification were made.

Dr. Barr then measured off a drop some ten or twelve inches shorter, and after a further protest Mr. Berry reluctantly agreed to go on with the job. Once again the reality of what happened has to be faced: the victim's head, although it did not actually come off, very nearly did so,[17] and this unfortunate fact was naturally one of the main subjects of discussion at the subsequent inquest.

17. *My Experiences as an Executioner*, p. 33.

At the inquest, of course, Mr. Berry was fully vindicated. And so, impliedly, was the use of quantitative methods in the noble science of hanging.

Suggestions for further reading

On Mr. Berry:
> *My Experiences as an Executioner*, by JAMES BERRY (ed. H. Snowden Ward, Lund & Co., 1892; reprinted by David & Charles, 1972)

On Hanging as a Science:
> *A Handbook on Hanging*, by CHARLES DUFF (republished as a Panther Book, 1956)

On Graphs:
> *Mathematician's Delight*, by W. W. SAWYER (Pelican Books, 1943), chapter 9

On Graphs of Linear and Curvilinear Functions:
> *Preface to Econometrics*, by M. J. BRENNAN (South-Western Publishing Co., 1965), chapter 2

Chapter 2
Was Malthus right about population after all?

*In which we study a modern version of the famous
Malthusian theory of population, thereby learning
more about the technical language in which the
fact of the interdependence of variables is
expressed, and building our first 'model'
of a social process.*

From our study of Mr. Berry's life and work we have learned
three things. First, we have learned how important it may be
to find out the exact way in which one quantity depends upon
or varies with another. Second, we have learned something
about the manner in which a hypothesis concerning the
quantitative relationship between two variables can be
formulated and tested. And third, we have learned quite a
lot about the different ways in which such a relationship can
be expressed—in a table, a graph, and an arithmetical
formula.

But, the reader may be objecting, no one today is interested
in becoming an efficient hangman. We are interested in understanding society. Let us turn, then, to an important
social problem—the problem of population—and see
whether the use of quantitative methods can throw any light
upon it.

The trouble here really started because Thomas Robert
Malthus, the begetter of the famous Malthusian theory of
population, did not like his father Daniel.

Nowadays sons rebel against their fathers because they
think they are too reactionary. In the last decade of the
eighteenth century they often rebelled against them because
they thought they were too progressive. Daniel Malthus, in
the eyes of his son Thomas Robert, was a dangerous radical
who had been infected by the wicked ideas of Godwin, and was
actually naïve enough to believe in the perfectibility of mankind. Something had to be done about it.

The first edition of T. R. Malthus's famous *Essay on
Population* (1798) took the form of an open attack upon those
who believed in 'the perfectibility of man and of society'. Its

main argument was as simple as it was sensational. Here it is in Malthus's own words:

'The power of population is indefinitely greater than the power in the earth to produce subsistence for man.

Population, when unchecked, increases in a geometrical ratio. Subsistence increases only in an arithmetical ratio. A slight acquaintance with numbers will show the immensity of the first power in comparison of the second.

By that law of our nature which makes food necessary to the life of man, the effects of these two unequal powers must be kept equal.

This implies a strong and constantly operating check on population from the difficulty of subsistence. This difficulty must fall some where; and must necessarily be severely felt by a large portion of mankind . . .

This natural inequality of the two powers of population, and of production in the earth, and that great law of our nature which must constantly keep their effects equal, form the great difficulty that to me appears insurmountable in the way to the perfectibility of society.'

This argument is chiefly founded on the proposition in the second paragraph—that population, when unchecked, 'increases in a geometrical ratio' (e.g., $1 + 2 + 4 + 8 + 16$, etc.), whereas subsistence 'increases only in an arithmetical ratio' (e.g., $1 + 2 + 3 + 4 + 5$, etc.). The 'geometrical ratio' Malthus took to be proved by the contemporary growth of population in North America. The 'arithmetical ratio' did not in his opinion really need any proof. 'Let us allow,' he says, 'that by great exertion, the whole produce of this Island might be increased every twenty-five years, by a quantity of subsistence equal to what it at present produces. The most enthusiastic speculator cannot suppose a greater increase than this.'

Now the process which Malthus is describing here is quite a complex one. On the one hand, he asserts, population increases (in a geometrical ratio) when subsistence increases. On the other hand, subsistence presumably increases (even if only in an arithmetical ratio) when population increases, since when population increases there will be an increase in the number of labourers capable of producing subsistence. So while population depends upon subsistence, subsistence at the same time depends to some extent upon population. Let us see whether we can sort out these two relations of dependence with the aid of the graphical techniques which we used in the last chapter.[1]

Just to simplify the problem, let us assume that we are dealing with an imaginary country which is isolated from the rest of the world, which has a fixed stock of land and capital, and which produces only one commodity which we shall call 'corn'—a kind of composite commodity that we take as a gauge of living standards.

Consider, first, the way in which population may depend upon subsistence. What Malthus says, to put it crudely, is that population will always tend to breed up to the minimum subsistence level. Let us assume that the minimum subsistence level is 5 bushels of 'corn' per person per year. The level of population, then, if Malthus is correct, will depend upon the total output of 'corn' which the country produces each year. If it produces nothing, the population will be zero. If it produces 5 bushels of 'corn' per year, the population will consist of 1 person. If it produces 10 bushels per year, the population will be 2 persons. If it produces 15 bushels per year the population will be 3 persons, and so on. In each case, the population will tend to be the maximum number consistent with each person receiving the assumed minimum subsistence of 5 bushels per year.

Let us draw a graph of this 'Malthusian' situation, then, measuring the number of persons in the population along the horizontal axis and the total amount of 'corn' produced per year (in bushels) up the vertical axis. If we put a dot in the appropriate place in the graph for each of the pairs of quantities described in the last paragraph, and join all the dots up, we will get an upward-sloping straight line like the one in Figure 2.1.

The line joining the dots shows us the *path* along which the population will increase as the output of 'corn' increases, after we have allowed sufficient time for the Malthusian principle to do its work. Suppose, for example, that we are at the moment at the dot labelled *A*, where output is 10 bushels and the population consists of 2 persons, each receiving the subsistence minimum of 5 bushels. Suppose now that for some

1. Much of the inspiration for what follows comes from Alan T. Peacock, 'Theory of Population and Modern Economic Analysis' (*Population Studies*, November 1962, pp. 114–122).

reason or other the output rises from 10 to 15 bushels per year, so that we move from point *A* to point *B*. Each of the 2 persons in the population will now be receiving $7\frac{1}{2}$ bushels per year—i.e., more than the subsistence minimum of 5—and on the Malthusian hypothesis the population will eventually

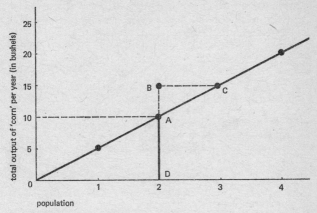

Figure 2·1

increase up to the point where output per head is again equal to 5 bushels. In other words, we shall sooner or later move from the point *B* to the point *C*, representing an output of 15 bushels and a population of 3 persons.

What does the *slope* of the line joining the dots measure? The degree of its slope can be worked out by taking any point on it—*A*, say—and dropping a vertical line *AD* from it to the base line of the graph. The slope will then be given by the ratio $\frac{AD}{OD}$. *AD* represents the total output of 'corn' at this point (10 bushels). *OD* represents the number of persons in the population (2). The slope $\frac{AD}{OD}$ therefore represents the minimum subsistence per head (5 bushels). If we assume that the slope remains the same throughout—i.e., that the line joining the dots is a *straight* line—then we are in effect assuming that people's ideas about what constitutes the minimum subsistence level (up to which they breed) do not alter as population increases. If people's ideas about this were in fact revised upwards as population increased, the line joining the dots would start curving upwards, whereas the opposite would be the case if they were revised downwards.

The line we have drawn shows us at a glance the way in which population depends upon or varies with output. The mathematicians would say that in this part of our exercise we were treating population as the *dependent variable* and output as the *independent variable*, and drawing a graph of the *functional* relation between them. Ordinary mortals think of a function as something which they either attend or perform. Mathematicians think of it in quite a different way. If they say that population is a function of output, what they mean is simply that population depends upon or varies with output, in such a way that if you know what output is you can immediately work out what population is. In our case, the number of persons in the population, after it has had time to adjust, is always equal to one-fifth of the number of bushels of 'corn' produced per year. Or, using a shorthand in which '*P*' stands for *P*opulation and '*C*' stands for the number of bushels of '*C*orn' produced per year, we have the simple functional relation

$$P = \tfrac{1}{5}C$$

Given this, if we know what *C* is we can readily calculate *P*.

Now consider, second, the way in which subsistence may depend upon or vary with population. The output of 'corn' does not come down like manna from heaven—it has to be *produced* by human effort. Thus the number of bushels of 'corn' produced per year will depend, in large part, upon the number of labourers who are available to produce it, and this will depend largely upon the number of people in the population.

What we must now do, therefore, is to treat subsistence as the dependent variable and population as the independent variable, rather than the other way round, and draw a graph of the functional relation between them. What is the most plausible assumption we can make about *this* functional relation—remembering that land and capital in our imaginary country are assumed to be fixed?

When population is low, so that there are relatively few labourers available, annual output will presumably also be low. As population increases, and more labourers become available to work the fixed stock of land and capital, annual output will also increase—at a relatively low rate at first, in all probability, but then at a more rapid rate. Sooner or later, however, if the stock of land and capital is truly fixed, the rate at which output increases with further increases in population will begin to fall off; and eventually there will come a point where there are so many labourers that they begin to get in one another's way, and further increases in population will be associated with an actual decline in output.

If this were the kind of relationship which existed between output (as the dependent variable) and population (as the independent variable), and we were able to draw a graph of it on a diagram in which (as before) we measured P along the horizontal axis and C up the vertical axis, how would we expect the relevant curve to behave? We would expect it to start at the origin of the graph, to go upwards first at an increasing rate and then at a declining rate, and eventually to reach a maximum and start going downwards. Let us assume that the actual relationship in the case we are considering is such that when graphed it comes out as in Figure 2.2.

We can now put this output-as-a-function-of-population curve in juxtaposition with the population-as-a-function-of-output line which we derived in Figure 2.1 on p. 29 above, and work out the level which the population of our imaginary country will *actually* reach if Malthus's theory is correct. Before we do this, however, it will be useful to ask what the *best* or 'optimum' level of population would be under these circumstances, so that we have a criterion with which to pass judgement on the *actual* level.

The answer we give to the question 'What is the optimum level of population?' will evidently depend upon how we *define* the optimum population. Suppose we say that it is the population at which total output per head is a maximum. Can we locate this level of population in Figure 2.2? We might be tempted at first to pick on OA, since the output-as-a-function-of-population curve reaches its maximum at B—i.e., at a population of OA. But a little thought will show us that this is wrong. What we want to find is not the population at which *total output* is a maximum, but that at which *total output per head* is a maximum.

We can use a cute little gimmick here. If we want to work

out total output per head at any point on the curve, the easiest
way to do it is to draw a straight line from the origin of the
graph (*O*) to the point concerned, and measure its *slope*. For
example, to work out total output per head at the point *D*,

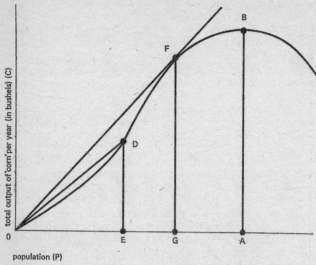

total output of corn per year (in bushels) (C)

population (P)

Figure 2·2

we draw a straight line from *O* to *D*. Its slope, measured in the
usual way, is DE/OE. Since *DE* is total output and *OE* is the
number of heads, the slope of *OD* represents total output per
head. To find the point on the curve where total output per
head is a maximum, therefore, all we have to do is to draw
straight lines from *O* to different points on the curve until we
hit on the line with the steepest possible slope. If the reader
imagines himself doing this, drawing a straight line from *O* to a
point on the curve just to the right of *D*, then to another point
just to the right of that, and so on, he will see that the slope of
the line gets steeper all the time until we reach the point *F*,
where the line drawn from *O* is just tangential to the curve.
This is the line of maximum steepness: after that the slope of
the lines will decline. Thus total output per head is at a maximum at the point *F*, and the optimum population in the
defined sense is *OG*.

With this criterion of what the population *ought* to be in our minds, then, let us now ask what the population in fact *will* be if Malthus's theory is correct. To answer this question we put our two basic diagrams together, as in Figure 2.3. The answer then leaps to the eye. The population will go on expanding

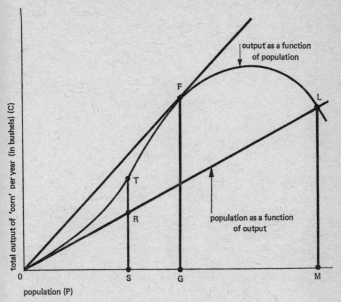

Figure 2·3

until it reaches the level represented by the point *M* on the base line of the graph, and there it will tend to stay. For suppose that the population were smaller than this—*OS*, say. The total output which will enable a population of *OS* to live at the minimum subsistence level of 5 bushels of 'corn' per year is given by the population-as-a-function-of-output line. Clearly it is *RS*. But the output which a population of *OS* will in fact produce is given by the output-as-a-function-of-population curve. It is *TS*, which is much greater than *RS*. Thus since the *OS* persons in the population will be receiving more than the subsistence minimum of 5 bushels per head, the population will tend to increase until it gets to *OM*, where the total output it produces (*LM*) will be just sufficient to give each person the subsistence minimum. If it happened to increase beyond *OM*, each person would receive less than the assumed subsistence minimum; some people would thereupon presumably cease to subsist; and population would eventually fall again. At *OM*, therefore, the population would be in a kind of equilibrium.

Note the appalling Malthusian moral of this. Population has bred up to subsistence with a vengeance. It has passed far beyond the optimum level *OG* at which *output per head* is a maximum; it has even passed beyond the point at which *output* is a maximum. And remember that it is kept at *OM* by the operation of certain highly unpleasant forces which Malthus called 'checks' and which he resolved into 'vice' and 'misery'.[2]

Well, there you are. Malthus *was* right about population after all. Or was he? Let us alter two of the assumptions we have so far been making and see what happens.

First, let us consider the assumption that capital and land are fixed in quantity. If this assumption were true, it would be reasonable to expect that the point at which the rate of increase in output started falling off, and the point at which output itself reached its maximum, would be reached relatively soon. But capital and land are *not* in fact fixed; nor is science. As population increases, capital may well be accumulated and the stock of at any rate *fertile* land may well be increased. This means, in effect, that every time population increases we really ought to draw a new output-as-a-function-of-population curve, higher than the previous one and reaching its maximum further to the right. So even if we assume that population does tend to breed up to the minimum subsistence level, moving steadily and inexorably up the population-as-a-function-of-output line, an equilibrium point like *L* in the diagram may never in fact be reached, because the output-as-a-function-of-population curve may move just as steadily ahead of it.

Second, let us consider the assumption that people's ideas about what constitutes the minimum subsistence level remain the same as output increases. The adoption of this assumption, as we have already seen (pp. 29–30), means that the functional relationship between population and output comes out as a

2. In later editions he added 'moral restraint', by which he did *not* mean birth control, but delayed marriage.

straight line. But suppose that the functional relation between population and output is not in fact a simple straight-line one. Suppose that when output increases beyond a certain point you get a continual upward revision of the subsistence minimum. People still 'breed up to the minimum of subsistence' in a certain sense, but their ideas as to what the 'minimum of subsistence' *is* are continually revised upwards. In that case the line on the graph will not go up in a straight line as in Figure 2.4, as we have so far assumed, but will bend back on itself as in Figure 2.5, indicating that in order to bring forth any given increase in population you now need a greater increase in output than you did before.

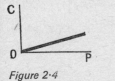
Figure 2·4

Figure 2·5

Let us draw a new picture, then, taking account as far as possible of these two new assumptions. So far as the output-as-a-function-of-population curve is concerned, since it would be rather difficult for us to cope with a constantly shifting curve, let us continue to assume that the stock of capital and land is fixed—but at a higher level than before, so that the curve reaches its maximum further to the right than it did before, and so that the point where total output per head is a maximum is also further to the right. So far as the population-as-a-function-of-output line is concerned, let us assume that after a point it now begins to curve upwards, so that it cuts the output-as-a-function-of-population curve further to the left than it did before. It is quite possible that we will then get something like the situation in Figure 2.6. The equilibrium level of population is still given by the point *L*, where the two curves intersect: it is clearly *OM*. But now, magically, *OM* is *less* than the optimum population *OG*. Now we have under-population, not over-population.

How has this result been arrived at? Starting from Malthus's premises, we seem to have reached a conclusion which is the exact reverse of the one which Malthus himself reached. The answer is that what we have actually done in the course of this instructive exercise is to *generalise* the original Malthusian theory. We have turned it into a much broader statement to the effect that the level of population will depend upon the interaction of two functions, one relating population to output, and the other relating output to population. The *actual* level of the population—and whether it is higher or lower than the *optimum* level—will depend upon the *form* or *shape* of these

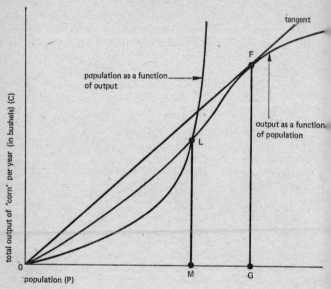

Figure 2·6

two functions. On the basis of one set of assumptions about their shape we will reach over-populationist conclusions, and on the basis of another set under-populationist ones.

And this leads me to the main moral I want to draw from all this—namely, that it may be very important in the case of real-world social problems to find out what the relevant functions *actually are*. The 'model' we have just been playing with, even as it stands, can certainly throw a considerable amount of light on some of the major issues involved in 'the population problem': in particular, it can help us to isolate and compare the general conditions which may lead either to over-population or to under-population. But the 'model' in itself does *not* enable us to predict which of these two things is in fact likely to happen in the case of any particular country, and therefore does not really help us to decide on the *policy* issues which may be involved. Suppose, for example, that the country concerned is an underdeveloped one, and that we are trying to work out the best method of assisting it. Should we send boat-loads of food to it, or should we encourage it to limit its population? To make up our minds about this, we would need to be able to draw the actual real-life curves—or, if you like, to ascertain the actual form or shape of the relevant functions. The next three chapters will be concerned with this crucial problem.

Suggestions for further reading

On the Model Discussed in This Chapter:
'Theory of Population and Modern Economic Analysis', by A. T. PEACOCK (*Population Studies*, November 1962, pp. 114–122)

On the Theory of Population:
General Theory of Population, by A. SAUVY

On the Economic Applications of Functions and Graphs:
Preface to Econometrics, by M. G. BRENNAN (South-Western Publishing Co., 1965), chapter 3

Chapter 3
How to regress in one easy lesson

In which, with the aid of an imaginary set of figures relating to income and consumption, we learn something about the philosophy and techniques of elementary regression analysis.

Enough has now been said in general terms about the different ways in which things may depend upon one another in the social sciences. We know now how important this dependence may be—whether one wants to be a hangman or a population expert—and we know something about the jargon in which the fact of dependence is expressed and the geometrical and arithmetical ways in which it can be represented. It is time to turn to the problem introduced at the end of the last chapter—how to find out what the functional relationships actually are in any particular case.

Mr. James Berry can give us some very helpful clues here, both in clarifying the nature of the problem which now faces us, and in working out a solution to it. When he came to frame his first hypothesis, Mr Berry's problem was this. He had only three observations of the proper relationship between length of drop and weight of client—two gained from actual observation ('Innes' and 'Vickers'), and one gained from intuition ('Basis'). What he wanted to do was to derive from this rather meagre set of observations the best possible estimate of the true underlying relationship between drop and weight. Given only the figures of the appropriate drops for clients of 9 stone 6 lb., 10 stone 4 lb., and 14 stone, he asked himself, what is the best possible estimate I can make of the drop required *for a client of any weight*?

The way in which he solved this problem, *in effect* (see Figure 3.1), was to draw a straight line through the dots, a line starting at the dot labelled 'Basis' and going up more or less midway between the other two. He felt instinctively that the best possible estimate he could make of the true underlying functional relationship between drop and weight was that it was the one embodied in this straight line, which in a sense seemed to 'fit the dots' better than any other.

Bearing all this in mind, let us proceed to develop Mr. Berry's technique a little and apply it to a completely new problem. We suspect, let us say, that there is some kind of functional relationship between the amount of *income* people receive and the amount of that income which they spend on

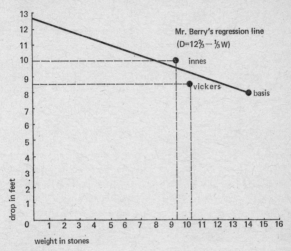

Figure 3·1

consumption goods.[1] As income increases consumption also increases—but how, exactly? What is the nature of the underlying relationship between these two variables? Can we put *figures* on this relationship, in such a way as to enable us to make the best possible estimate of what consumption will be at *any* given level of income?

Following in the footsteps of Mr. Berry, let us begin as he did and have a look (even if only in our imaginations) at the empirical data. There are two possibilities open to us here: either we can look at the figures for aggregate income and aggregate consumption over the country as a whole in different years; or we can look at the figures for the consumption of

1. This relationship—the so-called 'consumption function'—is a very important one in the field of economic theory and policy today. See the first reference under 'Suggestions for Further Reading' at the end of this chapter.

different groups of people with different incomes in any one year. In real life we would of course take a large number of pairs of observations: later on, in chapter 5, we shall discuss the question of how large a sample has to be in order to enable us to have confidence in the results we base on it. But in order to simplify the thing, let us suppose that we take only six observations, which come out like this:

Income (£m.)	Consumption (£m.)
1	2
2	1
3	2
4	4
6	5
8	4

Looking at these figures as they stand it is hard to make much sense out of them, or to see evidence of any underlying relationship between them. Maybe we can get a bit more enlightenment if we graph them, or plot them on a 'scatter diagram', to use the proper jargon, as is done in Figure 3.2.

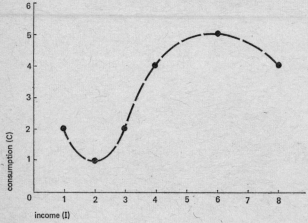

Figure 3·2

Looking at the six dots on this scatter diagram it would certainly appear that as income increases there is a tendency for consumption to increase as well. But this is hardly very surprising: it is no more than we could learn from common-sense. How do we start our task of deriving from the data the best possible estimate of the underlying relationship between the two variables?

Perhaps we should start by simply joining up all the points, to make a nice smooth curve like the dotted one in the diagram. Might this curve embody the true underlying relationship between income and consumption for which we are seeking? This would not seem to be very plausible. If the dotted curve *did* embody the true underlying relationship, we would have to accept as a fact that an increase in income would sometimes lead to an increase in consumption and sometimes to a decrease, which is hardly what we would expect in the real world. Possibly some of our figures are wrong.[2] Possibly some of them are not typical. Clearly we have made a false start and must begin again.

It is fairly obvious that under these circumstances the best we can hope to do is to arrive at some kind of *approximation* to the true underlying relationship. In the present case, it looks very much as if we could get a pretty fair approximation by drawing a straight line through the dots like the one in Figure 3.3. None of the dots are actually *on* this line, it is true, but they are spaced fairly evenly around it. Maybe we could take some more observations just to make sure: if most of the dots then fell inside a kind of narrow band sloping upwards more or less in a straight line, as in Figure 3.4, it would then seem even more likely that the underlying relationship between the variables was in fact a straight-line one.

So the problem in the case we are considering really boils down to the same kind of problem that Mr. Berry faced—to find the straight line which fits the dots best. If the dots had come out in the form of a curve, as in Figure 3.5, of course, the problem would have been to find the *curve* which fitted the dots best. Mr. Berry did this job too, in effect, when he formulated his second hypothesis. But we lesser mortals, not

2. The first pair of figures is not *necessarily* wrong, as might appear at first sight. If current income is very low, people may in fact spend an amount greater than their income on consumption goods—by drawing on past savings, getting into debt, selling valuables, etc.

being as clever as Mr. Berry, will stick to straight-line relationships for the time being.

What is the minimum amount of information we need about a straight line in order to be able to fix its position on a graph? The answer is that we need to know (*a*) the point where the line

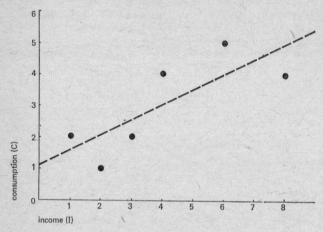

Figure 3·3

meets the vertical axis, and (*b*) the extent and direction of its slope.[3] Two illustrations should make this clear.

Take Mr. Berry's first hypothesis. The straight line corresponding to his first table intercepted the vertical axis at $12\frac{2}{3}$ ft., and went downwards to the right with a slope of 1 in 3, or $\frac{1}{3}$, as in Figure 3.6. The functional relation between the two variables which was embodied in this line was

$$D = 12\frac{2}{3} - \frac{1}{3}W$$

The $12\frac{2}{3}$ was the point where the line met the vertical axis; the $\frac{1}{3}$ was the slope of the line; and the sign between the $12\frac{2}{3}$ and the $\frac{1}{3}W$ was a minus rather than a plus because the line sloped downwards rather than upwards.

As a further illustration, take the relationship between Centigrade and Fahrenheit. To convert Centigrade into

3. See the Mathematical Appendix, section 10, pp. 216–17.

Fahrenheit, you have to multiply by 9, divide by 5, and add 32. In other words,

$$F = C \text{ multiplied by } \tfrac{9}{5} \text{ plus } 32$$

That is, $F = 32 + 1\tfrac{4}{5}C$

If we graph this relationship, measuring Centigrade along the horizontal axis and Fahrenheit up the vertical axis, we get a straight line which looks like that in Figure 3.7. It starts at 32 on the vertical axis; its slope is $1\tfrac{4}{5}$; and it slopes upwards.

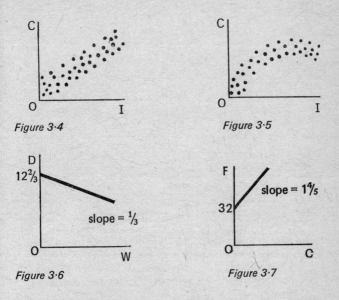

Figure 3·4

Figure 3·5

Figure 3·6

Figure 3·7

In both these cases, then, the position of the line on the graph is fixed by (*a*) the point where it meets the vertical axis, and (*b*) the extent and direction of its slope. In the arithmetical formula which the line embodies, the point where the line meets the vertical axis is given by the first figure on the right-hand side. The extent of the slope of the line is given by the second figure—the one by which the value of the independent variable has to be multiplied. And the direction of the slope is given by the sign in between these two figures: upward if it is a plus, downward if it is a minus.[4] If we know these two figures (the 'constants', as I shall call them), and the sign in between them, the position of the line on the graph is fixed.

All right then—what we are really looking for in the present case is values for these two 'constants' which will give us a straight line which in some significant sense fits the income/consumption dots better than any other straight line. And that leads us to another important question. What do we mean, exactly, by a line which fits the dots better than any other line? There are various possible ways of defining this, but the usual answer in the Statistics books is that it is a line for which the sum of the squares of the vertical distances by which the dots deviate from it is a minimum. This sounds so complex that we shall have to pause for a moment to put it into plain language.

In Figure 3.8, once again, is the scatter diagram which I drew in Figure 3.2 on p. 40 above, showing our six income/consumption dots and the straight line which I drew more or less arbitrarily through them in Figure 3.3. Now all the dots deviate vertically from the line by various distances which we can measure according to the scale we use on the vertical axis. These vertical deviations have been duly noted at the appropriate places on the graph. Suppose we now put all these deviations in a list, and side by side with them make out a list of the *squares* of the deviations. We would get the following:

Deviations	Squares of Deviations
+0·4	0·16
+0·9	0·81
+1·0	1·00
−1·1	1·21
−0·6	0·36
−1·0	1·00
	4·54 = sum of the squares of the deviations

4. It should be noted that the sign in between the figures is properly attributable to the second—i.e. the one representing the extent of the slope. In other words, the slope of Mr. Berry's line, strictly speaking, is *minus* $\frac{1}{3}$, and the slope of the Centigrade–Fahrenheit line is *plus* $1\frac{4}{5}$. See the Mathematical Appendix, section 10, p. 219.

The sum of the squares of the deviations in this case works out at 4·54. The line we are looking for, then—the 'line of best fit', the 'least squares line', or the 'regression line', as it is variously called—is simply the line for which the sum of the squares of the deviations, worked out in this way, is as small as it possibly can be.

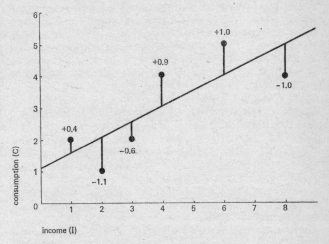

Figure 3·8

The reasons why we deal in terms of the sum of the *squares* of the deviations, rather than in terms of the simple sum of the deviations themselves, are purely technical. For example, the results you get when you use squares are technically more convenient when it comes to such matters as checking whether the number of observations in your sample is really sufficient to enable you to have confidence in your conclusions. A definition is merely a label—there is nothing sacrosanct about it—and we therefore choose, among a number of possible definitions which make sense, the one which is technically the most convenient.

At first sight it might seem as if we would now have to draw every possible line through the dots, adding up the squared deviations each time, and finally selecting the line for which the sum of the squares was a minimum. This would in fact take rather a long time, since the number of lines which we could draw through the dots (if we really tried) is infinitely large. It is therefore fortunate that a formula has been invented which enables us to get the right values for the two constants in a relatively short space of time without actually drawing any lines at all.

The way we do it, roughly speaking, is to set up two equations in which the two constants—which we shall call a and β respectively—appear as unknowns. We then get the right values for a and β by solving these equations. In the present case nothing much more than simple arithmetic and fourth-form algebra is required.[5] But the reader should not expect any of the steps in the calculation to make sense by itself. This is one of those cases in which we manipulate the figures in successive steps in a way that seems quite arbitrary, and then the right answer suddenly clicks out at the end. When doing this kind of operation I am always reminded of those complicated string figures where the manipulator twists the string in successive steps, so that everything seems to get more and more into a tangle, and then suddenly, at the end, there flashes out a seagull, or an eskimo house, or a string of diamonds.

The first thing to do is to set up an equation of the general form $C = a + \beta I$ for each of the six pairs of observations. We fill in the respective values for C and I in the case of each pair, but we leave the a's and β's as they are—they are the unknowns which we have to find. Then we add up the six equations, obtaining a kind of 'total' equation, which (in the present case) we can immediately simplify by dividing everything on both sides by 6. If we survive, we will emerge with the equation

$$3 = a + 4\beta$$

Then we set up another series of equations which are formed by multiplying each term in each of the equations in the first series by the appropriate value of I. Once again we leave the a's and the β's as they are; and once again we add up the six

5. The reader who has forgotten his fourth-form algebra will find all the necessary concepts and techniques explained in the first seven sections of the Mathematical Appendix.

equations to form a 'total' equation. When this is divided by 2, it simplifies to

$$44 = 12a + 65\beta$$

Calculation of least squares line

Income (I)	Consumption (C)	$C = a + \beta I$	$I(C = a + \beta I)$
1	2	$2 = a + \beta$	$2 = a + \beta$
2	1	$1 = a + 2\beta$	$2 = 2a + 4\beta$
3	2	$2 = a + 3\beta$	$6 = 3a + 9\beta$
4	4	$4 = a + 4\beta$	$16 = 4a + 16\beta$
6	5	$5 = a + 6\beta$	$30 = 6a + 36\beta$
8	4	$4 = a + 8\beta$	$32 = 8a + 64\beta$
	Sum of Equations:	$18 = 6a + 24\beta$	$88 = 24a + 130\beta$
		↓ (Divided by 6)	↓ (Divided by 2)
		(1) $\quad 3 = a + 4\beta$	(2) $44 = 12a + 65\beta$

Working

From (1), $a = 3 - 4\beta$

Substituting this value for a in (2), we get

$$44 = 12 (3 - 4\beta) + 65\beta$$
$$= 36 - 48\beta + 65\beta$$
$$\therefore 17\beta = 8$$
$$\therefore \boxed{\beta = +0\cdot4706}$$

Substituting this value for β in (1), we get

$$3 = a + 4(0\cdot4706)$$
$$\therefore \boxed{a = 1\cdot1176}$$

Conclusion: The least squares line starts at $1\cdot1176$ on the vertical axis and goes upwards at a slope of $0\cdot4706$.

Table 3·1

Table 3.1 shows how these equations are derived, and for good measure also shows how to solve them. a works out at $1\cdot1176$, which means that the least squares line starts at $1\cdot1176$ on the vertical axis. β works out at $+0\cdot4706$, which means that the line goes upwards[6] at a slope of $0\cdot4706$. This defines the line which will fit the dots better than any other line, in the sense that in the case of any other line the sum of

6. It goes upwards because the value of β is positive. If the value of β had been negative it would have gone downwards.

the squared deviations of the dots from it is bound to be greater than in the case of this line. *It can be proved* that this is so. By '*it can be proved*', I mean (*a*) that I cannot prove it myself, and (*b*) that I have implicit faith in those who claim that they can.

In the case of most real calculations, of course, the number of pairs of observations we took would be much greater than six, and if we had to do the whole thing by hand it would take us a long time. The coming of computers has effected a tremendous revolution in this respect. Any computer, provided we give it the proper instructions, will carry out all these complex operations for us in about two seconds flat.

The least squares line which we have worked out by this ingenious method provides us with the *best possible* estimate of the true underlying relations between income and consumption. It is the best possible basis, in other words, for predicting what consumption will be at any given level of income. But just because it is the *best possible* estimate, this does not necessarily mean that it is an estimate upon which we can safely rely.

Remember James Berry's first regression line. That line may have been the *best possible* estimate of the true underlying relation between drop and weight, given the information which was available. But clearly it was *not* an estimate upon which Mr. Berry should have relied.

Obviously we are not yet out of the wood. What we need now is some kind of quantitative measure of the *reliability* of the estimates embodied in our least squares line. Here the problem of *correlation* rears its ugly head, and demands a chapter to itself.

Suggestions for further reading

On the Consumption Function:

An Introduction to Positive Economics, by R. G. LIPSEY (Weidenfeld and Nicolson, 2nd Edn., 1966), chapter 43

On Regression Analysis

Use and Abuse of Statistics, by W. J. REICHMANN (Pelican Books, 1964), chapter 10 and appendix 3

A Primer of Social Statistics, by S. M. DORNBUSCH and C. F. SCHMID (McGraw-Hill Book Co., 1955), chapter 16

Chapter 4
How to correlate and identify

In which we meet the man who thought that milk-drinking was the cause of cancer, and learn something about the philosophy and techniques of elementary correlation and identification analysis.

There was once a man who believed that all the ills of the world were due to milk, and who set out to prove that milk-drinking was the cause of cancer. In the case of each of the hundred or so countries of the world for which the relevant statistics were available, he made a pair of observations of (*a*) the amount of milk consumed per head, and (*b*) the percentage of the population dying of cancer, in the year previous to that of his investigation. He then fed this data into a computer, which he programmed for a straight-line regression. The computer produced a least squares line which sloped upwards from left to right. 'There you are', said the man triumphantly, 'I told you so. Milk-drinking *is* the cause of cancer.'

What is wrong with this argument? First, the mere fact that the least squares line is upward-sloping does not necessarily mean that the relation between the two variables is an important or substantial one. What is relevant here is *the degree of closeness with which the observations approximate to the least squares line*.

Suppose, for example, that the relationship between the two variables came out on a scatter diagram as it does in Figure 4.1. There seems to be a general tendency here for the dots to move in an upward direction from left to right, but it is a pretty vague and shadowy tendency. If we tell the computer to fit a least squares line to the dots, however, it will in fact do so. There always must be a least squares line, and the computer will unerringly find it. It might, perhaps, be the line which I have had a shot at drawing in on the diagram.

But the individual dots deviate so much from this line, and so erratically, that we could have no confidence whatever in the line as a predictor. We would want to say in such a case that the relation between the two variables was not an

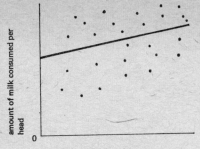

Figure 4·1

important or substantial one—meaning by this that although there appeared to be a general tendency for an increase in one to be associated with an increase in the other, the degree of closeness with which they moved together was very low.

Suppose, however, that the relationship between the two variables came out as it does in Figure 4.2. If this were the situation, the least squares line would obviously run straight through all the dots, and we would be prepared to place a great deal of reliance on the line as a predictor. We would want to say that in this case the relation between the variables *was* an important and substantial one—meaning by this that the degree of closeness with which they moved together was very high.

Most real-world cases, of course, would lie somewhere in between these two extremes, but our two examples have the merit of suggesting a way in which we could go about *measuring* the degree of closeness with which the variables were associated. We could do this by measuring *the degree of closeness with which the dots approximated to the fitted least squares line.*[1] Suppose, for example, that we could concoct a

1. We must be careful here. The degree of closeness with which the dots approximate to the fitted least squares line will *not* be an accurate measure of the degree of closeness with which the variables are associated *unless we have a sufficiently large number of dots.* Or, to put the same point in another way, the fewer the number of dots we have, the larger would the value given by the measure have to be before we could be reasonably sure that there was actually a significant relationship between the variables. The special problems involved here may become clearer after the reader has read Chapter 5, which deals with sampling theory.

measure which would give us an answer of, say, *one* in the
case we have just considered (where all the dots lay in a
straight line), and of, say, *zero* or something not far above it
in the previous case (where the dots were all over the place).

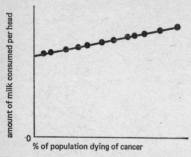

Figure 4·2

It would also be convenient if the measure gave us a *positive*
answer (somewhere between zero and *plus* one) in cases where
the dots went *up* from left to right, as in Figure 4.3, and a
negative answer (somewhere between zero and *minus* one) in
cases where they went *down* from left to right, as in Figure 4.4.

The statisticians have obligingly provided us with a measure
possessing precisely these qualities. Let us see what it is and
how it works by applying it to the set of imaginary figures

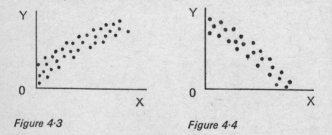

Figure 4·3   *Figure 4·4*

about income and consumption which we used in the last
chapter. Let us put these figures down once again in two
columns, and work out the *average* or *mean* values for income
and consumption respectively. This is hardly a very difficult

operation: we simply add up each of the columns and divide the total by the number of observations, i.e., by 6. The mean income works out at 4 and the mean consumption at 3.

Income	Consumption
1	2
2	1
3	2
4	4
6	5
8	4
6)24	6)18
Mean = 4	Mean = 3

Now most of the individual figures for income are either above or below the mean income of 4. In another column, headed *x*, we put down in the case of each figure the *amount* by which it deviates from this mean. Similarly, in another column, headed *y*, we put down the amount by which each of the consumption figures deviates from the mean consumption of 3. Then we multiply each *x* figure by the corresponding *y* figure, put the products in another column headed *xy*, and add them up.

Income	x	Consumption	y	xy
1	−3	2	−1	+3
2	−2	1	−2	+4
3	−1	2	−1	+1
4	0	4	+1	0
6	+2	5	+2	+4
8	+4	4	+1	+4
6)24		6)18	$\Sigma xy =$	+16
Mean = 4		Mean = 3		

The sum of the products of the individual *x*'s and *y*'s (for which the shorthand is Σxy) works out in this case at +16. It will work out as a positive quantity in all cases where increases in one variable are associated with increases in the other (i.e., where the dots go up from left to right). It will work out as a negative quantity in all cases where increases in one variable are associated with decreases in the other (i.e., where the dots go down from left to right). And it will work out at round about zero in all cases where there is little or no relationship between the variables (i.e., where the dots are all over the place).[2]

Σxy, then, seems to possess most of the qualities which we are looking for in our measure. But unfortunately it cannot be used as it stands: its value is not independent of the units in which we measure the variables, and it would be very unlikely to work out at one in the case where all the dots lay in a straight line. *It can be proved*,[3] however, that everything will come out all right in this respect if we divide Σxy by a number technically described as 'the geometric mean of the sums of the squared deviations'. This is not nearly as complex as it sounds, and the number can be worked out quite easily as follows:

x	y	x^2	y^2
-3	-1	9	1
-2	-2	4	4
-1	-1	1	1
0	$+1$	0	1
$+2$	$+2$	4	4
$+4$	$+1$	16	1
		$\Sigma x^2 = \overline{34}$	$\Sigma y^2 = \overline{12}$

Square each of the x's and total up the squares. Do a similar operation with the y's. Then multiply the two totals together and take the square root of their product. In the present case,

2. In the first of these three cases high values of the variables, and therefore positive x's and y's, will tend to be found together; similarly low values of the variables, and therefore negative x's and y's, will also tend to be found together. Σxy will therefore work out as a positive quantity. (Remember that the product of two negatives is a positive!) In the second case positive x's will tend to be found together with negative y's, and vice versa, so that Σxy will work out as a negative quantity. In the third case positive x's will tend to be found half the time with positive y's and half the time with negative y's; and similarly for negative x's. The minuses and pluses will more or less cancel one another out, and Σxy will be round about zero.

3. See p. 48 above for a definition of this expression.

the result works out at about 20·2. Dividing the value of +16 which we have already obtained for Σxy by this, we get a final value of +0·79 for what is called the *correlation coefficient*.[4]

The correlation coefficient (r in shorthand) gives us a measure of the extent to which the dots approximate to the fitted least squares *straight line*. It is important to note, therefore, that the particular method of working it out that I have just described should be used only in cases where the relationship between the variables is in fact a straight-line one.

There was once a man who investigated the relationship between health and exposure to the sun. He took a large number of pairs of observations and calculated r, which worked out at fairly near zero. 'All right,' said the man, 'there is clearly no connection at all between health and exposure to the sun, which means that I can expose myself to the sun for as long as I like.' So he lay on a Mediterranean beach in the middle of the summer for a very long time, and was unfortunately dead before anyone could explain to him the nature of his fallacy. Health and exposure to the sun are in fact related, but the relationship is curvilinear and not linear. If the man had plotted his pairs of observations on a scatter diagram they might have come out as they do in Figure 4.5, showing that after a certain point continuous exposure to the sun begins to cause a marked deterioration in health. What he *should* have measured was the extent to which the dots approximated to *a curve* of this type.

If he had done this—with the aid of more advanced techniques than those which I have described in this chapter—he would have found that there was a very high degree of correlation between the variables. But what he in fact measured was the extent to which the dots approximated to a straight line. And so he died.

Let us now return to our anti-milk man, who is bursting to tell us that he has just worked out r for his hundred-odd pairs of observations and has found that it is about +0·65. 'There you are,' he is saying, 'I was right after all. Milk-drinking *is* the cause of cancer.'

4. For those readers who prefer their arithmetic straight, the formula for the correlation coefficient is:

$$r = \frac{\Sigma xy}{\sqrt{(\Sigma x^2)(\Sigma y^2)}}$$

But this is where he falls into error for the second time. A high value for *r* would not necessarily mean that milk-drinking was the cause of cancer. To leap from *association* to *cause* in this way may involve us in the most awful fallacies. Take the

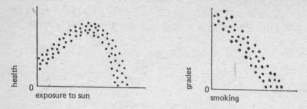

Figure 4·5   *Figure 4·6*

famous case of the relationship between examination grades and smoking.[5] Some investigators in America studied the relationship between these two variables, found that the dots went roughly as they do in Figure 4.6, and got a fairly high negative value for *r*. Does it follow from this, then, that smoking is the *cause* of low grades? Not necessarily. It *might* indicate the reverse—that low grades are the cause of smoking, since the unfortunate students who get low grades are driven to smoking in order to console themselves. More probably, perhaps, the mutual association between the variables can be explained by the fact that both are a product of some third thing. For example, it may be that sociable students who take their studies lightheartedly are also likely to smoke more. Or perhaps it has something to do with the difference between extroverts and introverts. Extroverts, it seems, tend to get lower grades than introverts—and maybe extroverts smoke more than introverts.

Having pondered on these possibilities, the reader may like to have a go himself at explaining the two picturesque cases illustrated in Figures 4.7 and 4.8, in each of which there is said to be a high degree of correlation between the variables concerned.[6] Armed with his analysis of these examples, he

5. My description of this case is modelled on that in chapter 8 of *How to Lie with Statistics*, by Darrell Huff (Victor Gollancz, 1954), in which a number of other choice examples will be found.

6. The figures are supposed to be scatter diagrams in which each point indicates the values of the two variables concerned in a particular year.

should then fairly easily be able to turn upon the unfortunate anti-milk man and rend him limb from limb.[7]

One important moral to be drawn from all this is that the job of quantifying social relations is by no means an easy one. The unwary practitioner of social arithmetic is faced with a whole number of pitfalls. I want now to say a little about quite a different one, which I myself always find equally interesting

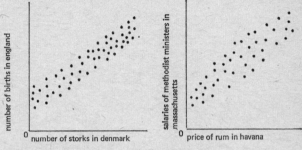

Figure 4·7   Figure 4·8

and spectacular. This is the fact that the curve you get as a result of the application of regression techniques may not in fact be the one you are looking for at all, but an absolutely different one. This involves us in what the statisticians call the *problem of identification*.

Once again I shall illustrate the problem with a story—but this time it will be a perfectly true one. There was once an econometrician called Moore who set out to find the *demand curves* for two representative commodities, corn and pig iron. As everyone who has looked through a book on economics will know, a *demand curve* shows the way in which the amount of a commodity demanded by purchasers per unit of time (per month, say) varies as the unit price of the commodity varies, other things remaining equal. Normally, of course, more of a commodity is purchased when its price falls, and less when its price rises, so that if we measured demand along the horizontal axis of a graph and price up the vertical axis we would expect the dots to go downwards from left to right. Moore, however,

7. He will obtain some useful assistance here from *How to Lie with Statistics*, pp. 95–6.

upon applying quantitative techniques which were very advanced for his day, found something very surprising.

In the case of corn, everything was normal enough: the dots went down from left to right as they do in Figure 4.9. In the case of pig iron, however, they went *up* from left ro right, as they do in Figure 4.10. This was an extraordinary result, but Moore had the courage of his convictions. He fitted least

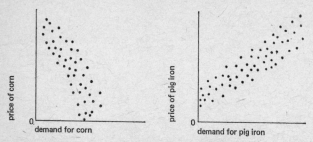

Figure 4·9   *Figure 4·10*

squares lines to both sets of dots, proclaimed them to be approximations to 'the' demand curves for corn and pig iron respectively, and sat back to see what the economists would say about the pig iron case.

This caused quite a bit of fluttering in the economic dove-cotes, until a wise gentleman called (appropriately) Working spotted what was wrong. The dots on Moore's diagrams, he said, all presumably represented the crossing-points of demand and supply curves; and obviously these curves must have moved about quite a bit during the half-century or so covered by Moore's observations.[8] In the corn case, the

8. Those readers who have no knowledge of economics may like a few words of explanation here. Just as we can draw a *demand* curve showing the way in which the *demand* for a commodity will vary with its price, other things remaining equal, so we can also draw a *supply* curve (see Figure 4.12) showing the way in which the *supply* of a commodity will vary with its price, other things remaining equal. The *equilibrium* price of the commodity will tend to be that at which the amount demanded by consumers is equal to the amount supplied by producers. If the curves are those in Figure 4.13, for example, the equilibrium price will be *OP* and the equilibrium amount demanded and supplied will be *OM*. Suppose now that consumers' incomes increase, so that they demand more of the commodity at any given price than they do now. The

demand curves had probably moved very little, but the supply curves had moved a lot, as in Figure 4.11, so that the least squares line fitted to the dots represented by the crossing-points of the demand and supply curves was in fact an approximation to 'the' demand curve.

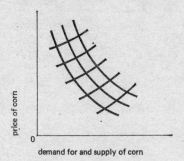

Figure 4·11

In the pig iron case, on the other hand, the supply curves had probably moved very little, but the demand curves had moved a lot, as in Figure 4.14, so that the least squares line

---

demand curve will then shift to the right—to D^1, perhaps—and a new equilibrium price of OP^1 and a new equilibrium amount demanded and supplied of OM^1 will be established. Similarly, if anything happens to change the amount supplied at any given price—an alteration in costs

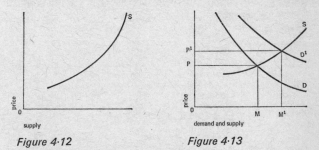

Figure 4·12　　　　　　　　*Figure 4·13*

of production, for example—the supply curve will shift and a new equilibrium price and amount will be established. This account begs a dozen questions, but it will do to be going on with.

fitted to the dots was in fact an approximation not to 'the' demand curve *but to 'the' supply curve.*[9]

This seems a very plausible explanation. In agriculture, the supply curves are in fact likely to move a lot, owing to changes

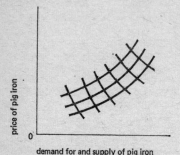

Figure 4·14

in the weather, and so on. In producers' goods industries, on the other hand, the demand curves are likely to move a lot, owing to the big fluctuations in demand for such goods which occur during booms and slumps.

So we can all sleep easily in our beds: the demand curve for pig iron, in all probability, behaves normally after all. But whenever there is a possibility of something like Moore's Mistake occurring, the social scientist has to be on the lookout. As usual, the statisticians have invented techniques for getting over this 'identification problem'. Fortunately or unfortunately, these techniques are a little too esoteric for us to absorb at this stage in our quantitative careers.

9. Whence, of course, the old song:

> *Said Moore: 'Goodness gracious! Oh my!*
> *This demand curve is sadly awry.'*
> *'Not so,' replied Working,*
> *'A fallacy's lurking:*
> *It isn't demand—it's supply.'*

Suggestions for further reading

On Correlation:

How to Lie with Statistics, by DARREL HUFF (Victor Gollancz, 1954), chapter 8

Use and Abuse of Statistics, by W. J. REICHMANN (Pelican Books, 1964), chapter 10 and appendix 1

A Primer of Social Statistics, by S. M. DORNBUSCH and C. F. SCHMID (McGraw-Hill Book Co., 1955), chapter 17

On Demand and Supply Analysis:

An Introduction to Positive Economics, by R. G. LIPSEY (Weidenfeld and Nicolson, 2nd Edn., 1966), chapters 17–19

On Moore's Mistake:

'What do Statistical "Demand Curves" Show?', by E. J. WORKING (reprinted in the American Economic Association's *Readings in Price Theory*, Allen and Unwin, 1953)

On the Problem of Identification:

Preface to Econometrics, by M. J. BRENNAN (South-Western Publishing Co., 1965), chapter 23

Chapter 5
Are students revolting?

In which we make an imaginary inquiry into students' political beliefs, and are thereby introduced to elementary sampling theory and technique.

Let us suppose that we want to get an accurate idea of the political opinions of university students in Great Britain. We begin, let us say, by devising a numerical scale on which to measure these opinions—a scale which goes from zero for extreme right-wing attitudes to, say, 50 for extreme left-wing attitudes. We then concoct an ingenious questionnaire, the replies to which will enable us to place each student who answers it at some specific point between zero and 50 on our scale. And we then proceed to send this questionnaire to students, or to approach them personally with it.

This is the point at which the famous 'sampling problem'—perhaps the most ubiquitous quantitative problem in the whole field of the social sciences—comes into the picture. There are, let us say, 250,000 students in Great Britain. It would be very nice if we could present our questionnaire to the whole lot of them, because we would then be certain that the answers (provided all the students in fact gave answers) were truly representative. But it is unlikely that we will in fact be able to do this. Because of considerations of cost, or convenience, or practicality, or time, we will probably be able to approach only a relatively small number of students. Let us suppose that we are in fact able to approach no more than 100. Two major problems now arise.

The first problem is how to avoid bias in the selection of our sample of 100. If we want the sample to be really representative of the whole student population, as we presumably do, it must be a truly *random* sample, in the sense that every student in the country has an equal chance of being selected. How would we go about ensuring this? Ideally, in order to make the sample absolutely random in this sense, we ought to assign a serial number to each of the 250,000 students, put 250,000 balls with these numbers on them into a gigantic receptacle, mix them very thoroughly, draw out 100 of them at random, and select the 100 students whose names correspond to the chosen numbers. And even this would not be enough for some statistical purists, who insist that the human element must be removed completely from the process of selection. The selection of our sample, they argue, must not be left to a human being picking balls out of an urn, but must be committed to an impersonal machine, or to a table of random numbers.

But all this is a counsel of perfection. Clearly it would be very difficult to do anything so elaborate with a population[1] as large as 250,000. Some kind of compromise method would have to be adopted. One possible way would be to put the names of all the 250,000 students down in an enormous list, to start at a point chosen at random, and to select every 2,500th name. We would have to be careful even here, of course, to ensure that the list was not arranged in such a way as to give students holding any particular point of view a greater chance of turning up at every 2,500th place.

There is really no short cut if we want to make sure that our sample is truly representative. It would be no good, for example, selecting one university at random and concentrating on that: we might get the London School of Economics, or, at the other extreme—I shall have to be very careful here—St. Andrews. It would be no good sending girls with our questionnaires to, say, 10 universities chosen at random, and asking them to approach 10 students chosen at random in each of them. The 10 universities selected might include Oxford and Cambridge; and on some campuses there might be special reasons—a sit-in, say, or a visit from Mr. Enoch Powell—why large numbers of students of one political viewpoint happened to be around on that day. And it would not be much good telling our girls to interview, say, so many men, so many women, so many people with long hair, so many with short hair, so many well-dressed people, so many badly-dressed people, and so on. Even if we took great care to make the numbers in these categories correspond to the numbers in the student population as a whole, the human element would come in far too heavily for comfort. Even assuming that the

1. I use the word 'population' in this chapter in the special sense in which it is used in Statistics books. It means simply the entire group from which the sample is chosen—in this case the 250,000 students in Great Britain.

girls made serious attempts to obey our instructions—which in itself is very difficult to ensure—opinions might well differ widely as to whether a particular student had long hair or short hair, was well dressed or badly dressed, or even whether he was a man or a woman.[2]

All right—we just do the best we can with this one. We take all *possible* precautions against the intrusion of bias, give our interviewers (if we decide to employ them) instructions which are as clear as we can make them, get our sample of 100 students selected, and keep our fingers crossed.

There is one thing about which we have to be clear, prefer- ably before we devise our questionnaire and certainly before we start analysing the answers, and that is the particular aspect or aspects of students' political opinions which we want to investigate. We might be interested, for example, in the numbers of students holding *extreme* political views—e.g., in the numbers whose answers put them in the 0–10 range on the score sheet, or in the 40–50 range. We might be interested in the extent to which political attitudes were *spread out* over the whole spectrum. Or we might be interested simply in the *average* or *mean* score, which could perhaps be taken as reflecting the opinion of the 'average student'. To simplify things, let us assume that it is only this last aspect in which we are in fact interested.

It is at this point that the second problem—which will take us rather longer to deal with than the first—comes in. We have chosen our sample of 100 students; they have answered the questions in our questionnaire; we have translated their answers into scores ranging from zero to 50; and we have worked out the *mean* score[3] of the 100 students in our sample, which turns out to be, say, approximately 30. On the basis merely of the fact that the mean score of the 100 students in our sample is 30, what if anything can we say about the mean score which we would have got if we had been able to send our questionnaire to *all* the 250,000 students in the popula- tion? What can we say, in other words, about the political

2. All this is not to say, of course, that the results of a survey can never be improved by purposive selection, if sufficient information is already available.

3. By the *mean* score, I mean simply the 'average' score in the gener- ally accepted sense—i.e. the sum total of all the 100 scores, divided by 100.

attitudes of the 'average student' *in Great Britain as a whole* on the basis merely of the political attitudes of the 'average student' *in our sample of 100*?

At first sight, it might seem that we could in fact say nothing at all. The single sample of 100 which we have taken, although it may be a perfectly random one, is very small indeed relative to the total population of students. It may well include—quite by accident—an unduly large number of students with political opinions at one or other of the two extreme ends of the scale. If that were so, the mean score of our sample would be appreciably above, or appreciably below, the true mean score of the population of students as a whole. And this is indeed always possible. But even though it is *possible*, it may or may not be very *probable*, and a kindly Providence has so ordained it that we are able to predict the *extent* of its probability. This, as I shall show more clearly in a moment, makes all the difference. It allows us, merely on the basis of the fact that the mean score of a single sample of 100 students is, say, 30, to make remarkably definite statements about the true mean score of the population of students as a whole. It does not, of course, enable us to say what this true mean score actually is: that would be too much to expect, even of Providence. But we can make pretty precise statements of a probabilistic character about it. We may be able to say, for example, something like this: 'It is 99% probable that the true mean score of the population lies within a range of two points on either side of the sample mean score of 30.' And for all practical purposes this may well be enough.

Let me now explain in more detail the particular dispensations of Providence which enable us to reach this remarkable result, and show how we would go about making the relevant calculations in the case we are taking as our example.

The best way to explain the basic philosophy of the thing is this. We have assumed, quite realistically, that we are able to take only *one* sample of 100 students out of the population of 250,000, and that the mean score of this single sample of 100 is all that we have to go on. But let us now, for the sake of the argument, make the highly unrealistic assumption that we are in fact able to take *a very large number* of separate samples of 100 students each out of the population. Let us imagine that we have taken and now have in front of us the scores of, say, 10,000 randomly-chosen samples of 100 students each.

And let us imagine that we work out the mean score of each sample, and put the 10,000 mean scores down in a list. We would find, presumably, that these mean scores would vary over quite a wide range, depending on the relative numbers of students of different political opinions who happened by chance to be included in the sample concerned. In the case of some of the samples the pattern of political opinions of the students included in them would correspond to the overall pattern in the student population as a whole, so that the mean score of these samples would be the same as the true mean score of the population. In the case of other samples, in which a greater number of left-wing students happened by chance to be included, the mean scores of the samples would be greater than the true mean score of the population, by varying amounts. In the case of yet other samples, in which a greater number of right-wing students happened to be included, the mean scores of the samples would be less than the true mean score of the population, again by varying amounts.

Now the truly remarkable thing about this is that although we do not—and probably could not—in fact take this very large number of samples and work out their mean scores, the laws of probability enable us to predict pretty accurately one very important feature of the result we would get if we did. *They enable us to predict the way in which the mean scores of the 10,000 samples would be grouped or distributed around the true mean score of the population.* To be more specific, they enable us to make a set of statements about the percentages of the mean scores of the samples which would lie within certain defined distances on either side of the true mean score of the population. The unit in which these distances are measured will be discussed more fully in a moment: in the meantime let us simply call it '*D*' for *D*istance. What we are able to say, in concrete terms, is that the mean scores of 68·26% of the samples would lie within *one* of these *D*-units on either side of the true mean score of the population; that the mean scores of 95·44% of them would lie within a distance *twice* as great as this (i.e., 2*D*) on either side of the true mean score of the population; and that the mean scores of 99·73% of them would lie within a distance *three* times as great as this (i.e., 3*D*) on either side of the true mean score of the population[4].

4. *It can be proved* that this is so. Readers who are not content to take this on trust should consult one of the Statistics textbooks listed at

This may be a bit clearer if we put it in the form of a diagram:

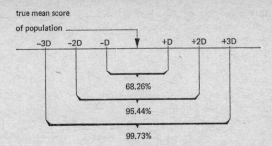

true mean score

of population

-3D   -2D   -D   +D   +2D   +3D

68.26%

95.44%

99.73%

All right—but so what? This information, fairly obviously, will be of no use at all to us unless we are able to estimate the value of *D* (in terms of points on our 0–50 scale). And the difficulty here is that *D* is not and cannot be a fixed amount which is the same in all cases. A moment's thought will show that its value must depend on the extent to which the political opinions of the whole population of students happen to be spread out over the spectrum.[5] But *we do not know* how the political opinions of the whole population of students are spread out. In fact we do not know anything at all about the opinions of the whole population: it is precisely in order to find out something about them that we have taken our single sample of 100. How can these pretty predictions help us, then? If we try to use them, will we not get ourselves caught up in a vicious circle?

Fortunately, the statisticians have shown that it is possible to deduce the spread of the political opinions of the whole

the end of this chapter. The same goes for the derivation of the formula on p. 68.

5. If the reader cannot see this, let him consider for a moment the fact that according to the theory 99·73%—i.e., virtually all—of the mean scores of our 10,000 samples would lie within a distance of '3*D*' on either side of the true mean score of the population. Suppose that there were hardly any students in the population with extreme scores in, say, the 0–10 and 40–50 ranges. The mean scores of our 10,000 samples would then lie within a smaller distance on either side of the true mean score of the population than they would do if there were in fact appreciable numbers of students with scores in the two extreme ranges. '3*D*', and therefore '*D*' itself, would thus be smaller in the first case than in the second.

population, with a fair degree of accuracy, from their spread in the single sample we have taken. This means that we are in fact able to work out a pretty reliable figure for the value of *D on the basis of the characteristics of our single sample*. A relatively simple short-cut formula which we can use for this purpose is the following:

$$D = \frac{\sqrt{\Sigma x^2}}{n}$$

Here '*D*' is the *D*istance we are looking for; '*x*' is the extent to which each of the individual scores in our single sample deviates from the mean score of the sample; '$\sqrt{\Sigma x^2}$' is the square root of the sum of the squares of these individual deviations; and '*n*' is the number of students in our sample— i.e., 100 in the particular case we are considering.

The first thing we must do, then, is to study the individual scores in our sample and work out the value of $\sqrt{\Sigma x^2}$. This is a laborious but not essentially difficult job. To illustrate how it is done, let us assume for the sake of simplicity that the scores in our sample of 100 are distributed in the following rather unlikely way:

	Total scores
9 students have a score of 20	180
17 students have a score of 25	425
49 students have a score of 30	1470
18 students have a score of 35	630
7 students have a score of 40	280
Total = 100	Total = 2985

The mean score of the sample works out at 29·85, which is near enough to the mean score of 30 which we have assumed for our sample.

We can now calculate the value of $\sqrt{\Sigma x^2}$ quite simply. In the case of the first group of 9 students, each of their scores deviates by -10 from the mean score of (approximately) 30. Thus in their case *x* is -10 and x^2 is 100, so that the group as a whole contributes a total of $9 \times 100 = 900$ to Σx^2. In the case of the second group of 17 students, each of their scores deviates by −5 from the mean score. Thus in their case *x* is −5 and x^2 is 25, so that the group as a whole contributes a total of $17 \times 25 = 425$ to Σx^2. The third group of 49 students contributes zero (since their scores do not deviate at all from the mean score); the fourth group of 18 contributes 450; and the fifth and last group of 7 contributes 700. Thus Σx^2 is $900 + 425 + 0 + 450 + 700 = 2,475$, which for our purposes is near enough to 2,500. Thus $\sqrt{\Sigma x^2} = 50$.

To work out the value of *D* in this case, therefore, we simply substitute 50 for $\sqrt{\Sigma x^2}$ and 100 for *n* in our basic formula

$$D = \frac{\sqrt{\Sigma x^2}}{n}$$

So *D* works out at 50/100, i.e., at 0·5 of a point. Bearing in mind the prediction set out on p. 66, then, we could be certain that if we took a very large number of samples, the mean scores of 68·26% of them would lie within a range of 0·5 of a point on either side of the true mean score of the population; that the mean scores of 95·44% of them would lie within a range of 1 point (i.e., 2*D*) on either side of it; and that the mean scores of 99·73% of them would lie within a range of 1·5 points (i.e., 3*D*) on either side of it.

We are now ready for the final step. We have deduced that if we took a very large number of samples—10,000, say—the mean score of 9,973 of them (i.e., 99·73%) would lie within a range of 1·5 points on either side of the true mean score of the population. Or, to put this in another way, we have deduced that if we took a single sample there is a 99·73% probability that its mean score would lie within a range of 1·5 points on either side of the true mean score of the population. Well, we *have* taken a single sample, and its mean score is 30: therefore we can say that it is 99·73% probable—i.e., virtually certain—that this figure of 30 lies somewhere within a range of 1·5 points on either side of the true mean score of the population. Knowing this, it is easy to work out the range within which the true mean score itself must lie. The sample mean score of 30 cannot be more than 1·5 points *greater* than the true mean score; therefore the true mean score cannot be more than 1·5 points *less* than 30. And the sample mean score of 30 cannot be more than 1·5 points *less* than the true mean score; therefore the true mean score cannot be more than 1·5 points *greater* than 30. Thus the true mean score must lie within a range of 1·5 points on either side of the sample mean score of 30. This is not a very wide range—a total of only 3 points in a scale of 50 points—and when one comes to think about it, it is rather remarkable that we can say anything as precise as this about the characteristics of a population of 250,000 merely on the basis of a single sample of 100.

It is true, of course, that we cannot claim that this result is absolutely certain—merely that it is 99·73% probable. We *might* conceivably have been unlucky enough to get a very exceptional sample, in which case the true mean score might in fact lie outside the range indicated by our result. But since such a thing would happen only in the case of 27 samples out of 10,000, this degree of probability would be high enough for most people. (If there is any doubt, of course, we can always take another sample and check up.) In fact many people would be prepared to accept a slightly lower degree of probability, and be content to say, e.g., that it is 95·44% probable that the true mean score lies within a range of one point (i.e., $2D$) on either side of the sample mean score of 30.

You will notice that we cannot reduce the size of the range without at the same time reducing the probability that the true mean score does in fact lie within it. We could of course take a larger sample, thereby reducing the value of D, but this is not quite as easy a way of getting out of the difficulty as we might think. For in order to reduce the size of D—and therefore the size of the range—by, say, one-half, we would have to quadruple the size of the sample.[6]

Finally, a few words of warning. The results which we

---

6. In the case we have been considering, $n = 100$ and $\Sigma x^2 =$ approximately 2,500, so that $D = \frac{\sqrt{\Sigma x^2}}{n} = \frac{\sqrt{2,500}}{100} = 0·5$. If one raises n from 100 to 200, the number of x's will double and Σx^2 will therefore rise to approximately 5,000. D will then be $\frac{\sqrt{5,000}}{200}$, i.e., 0·35. Doubling n, it will be seen, has *not* halved D. In order to halve D, one must quadruple n, since only then, when $n = 400$ and $\Sigma x^2 = 10,000$, will D fall to 0·25. This calculation, incidentally, gives us an idea of how we ought to proceed if the 'sampling problem' confronts us in the following, rather different, form: 'What should the size of my sample be if I want to be able to say that the true mean lies within a specified range of, say, 0·75 points, with a probability of, say, 99·73%?' The answer in the present case is 1,600.

derive by the method I have just described may be statistically correct, but before we actually use them as the basis for policy proposals there are a number of hazards of which we should be aware.

First, the mean score which we have obtained may be pretty useless by itself. In order to get a proper picture of the total situation, we may also want to know how students' political opinions are distributed around this mean, what proportion of them fall into the different score categories, and so on. And to obtain this kind of information about the population, on the basis of the characteristics of a single sample, would entail the use of methods which differ in detail—though not in principle—from that described above.

Second, we should look carefully into the question of how many of the students whom we originally selected actually answered the questionnaire. If some of them did not answer it at all, we are in a bit of a dilemma. If we do *not* substitute other students for them our result may well be badly biased, because apathetic students who do not answer questionnaires will not be adequately represented in our sample. And if we *do* substitute other students for them, then unless we do this very carefully our result may still be biased, because we are in effect interfering with the basic method of random selection with which we started.

Third, there may be a bias in our results due to the nature of some of the questions in our questionnaire. For example, it would certainly be reasonable, in a questionnaire designed to reveal political attitudes, to include a question or two about the journals read by the student concerned. But experience has shown that people tend to fit their answers to such questions to what they believe to be the accepted conventional code of conduct in the circles in which they move. If this factor is likely to be important, some way of checking up will have to be devised.

Fourth, if we use interviewers we should remember that the answers given may depend on the person who is doing the interviewing. The answers given to a pretty girl may be very different from those given to an ugly man. And American surveys have shown that the answers given by black interviewees to certain sensitive questions may vary greatly according to the colour of the interviewer.

Fifth and finally, we should not take the results of our survey as necessarily reflecting some innate and permanent character-istic of the student population. The results obtained during or just before a wave of sit-ins may be very different from those obtained in the period of reaction that may follow. Also the results of one survey, if published, may well affect the results of a later one.

Sampling, then, is like free will: the only arguments about it that one can think of are arguments against it. But just so that we should not leave this chapter in too sceptical a mood, let me finish with a story.

There was once a man who did not believe in sampling, and who campaigned against it up and down the country. He emphasised all the dangers I have just emphasised myself, pointing out in particular that sampling was necessarily based on probabilities rather than on certainties, so that you could never really be *sure* that your conclusions were correct. One day he was due to give a lecture on the evils of sampling in a nearby town. He got up, and went down to breakfast. His egg did not look too good, so he tasted a bit of it, found that it seemed all right, and finished the lot. He put his hand outside the door, felt that it was raining, and decided to take an umbrella. He looked in the rack for a magazine to read in the train, thumbed through one or two, found one that looked interesting, and put it in his pocket. When the train pulled into the station he chose the carriage that looked the cleanest, and travelled to the nearby town. He went to the lecture hall, and gave his anti-sampling lecture, which was received with rapturous applause by an audience of about a hundred people. 'How did it go?', his wife asked him when he got home again. 'Wonderful, wonderful,' the man replied, 'it's obvious that there's a very strong feeling in the country against sampling.'

Suggestions for further reading

On Sampling:

How to Lie with Statistics, by DARRELL HUFF (Victor Gollancz, 1954), chapter 1

Use and Abuse of Statistics, by W. J. REICHMANN (Pelican Books, 1964), chapters 16–19

A Primer of Social Statistics, by S. M. DORNBUSCH and C. F. SCHMID (McGraw-Hill Book Co., 1955), chapters 9–15

Preface to Econometrics, by M. J. BRENNAN (South-Western Publishing Co., 1965), chapters 17–19

Chapter 6
Underdeveloped models

In which we examine more thoroughly the concept of a 'model' in the social sciences, with the aid of two 'models' of particular relevance to the problems of underdeveloped countries.

Let us review the troops. We have applied our *regression* techniques and got a least squares line. We have checked that the degree of *correlation* between the variables is sufficiently high to enable us to rely on the predictions embodied in the line. We have carried out the necessary *identification* tests to make sure that we have in fact got the line we were looking for. And we have used *sampling theory* to check up that the number of observations we have made is sufficient. We are now ready to use the line as a building-block in the construction of socio-economic *models*.

There are numerous definitions of a 'model' to choose from in the books. In the broad sense in which I am using the term here, a 'model' is simply the formal expression—whether in words, diagrams or equations—of some basic underlying relationship or set of relationships between important socio-economic variables. In this chapter I shall be concerned mainly with models in which *two* different relationships, each embodied in a separate line or curve, are combined together—as they were, for example, in the case of the population—output model in chapter 2.

The first model I want to discuss has as its basis the simple demand–supply analysis outlined in chapter 4. Let us imagine that we have worked out the *actual* demand and supply curves for a particular commodity, and that we have drawn them on a graph (Figure 6.1). We assume—if only because our techniques at the moment are not up to anything else—that the curves come out as straight lines. The demand curve, let us say, starts at 14 on the vertical axis, and slopes downwards with a slope of 1 : 1, i.e., its slope is 1. This means, as we already know, that the relation between the variables can be expressed in the form of the equation

$$P = 14 - D$$

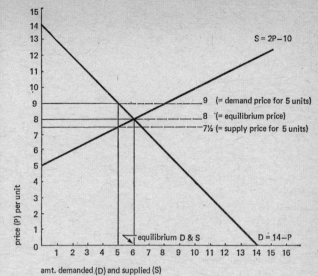

Figure 6·1

where '*P*' stands for *P*rice and '*D*' for *D*emand. Or, putting this round the other way to show demand as a function of price, we have

$$D = 14 - P \qquad . \quad . \quad . \quad . \quad . \quad . \quad . \quad (1)$$

The supply curve, let us say, starts at 5 on the vertical axis and slopes upwards with a slope of 1 : 2, i.e., its slope is $\frac{1}{2}$. The appropriate equation on the supply side is therefore

$$P = 5 + \tfrac{1}{2}S$$

or, putting it round the other way,

$$S = 2P - 10 \qquad . \quad . \quad . \quad . \quad . \quad . \quad . \quad (2)$$

It is very easy now, of course, to work out the *equilibrium* price—the price, that is, at which the amount supplied and the amount demanded are equal. We can get it directly, if we want to, by simply looking at the diagram. There is only one price at which the amount supplied and the amount demanded are equal, and that is the price opposite the point at which the two curves intersect—the price of 8. At this price, 6 units of the commodity will be demanded and 6 units will be supplied.

Or we can get it, almost as simply, with the aid of the two equations above which I have marked (1) and (2):

$$D = 14 - P \qquad \ldots \ldots \ldots \ldots \ldots (1)$$
$$S = 2P - 10 \qquad \ldots \ldots \ldots \ldots \ldots (2)$$

Since we know that in equilibrium D must equal S, we can immediately put

$$14 - P = 2P - 10$$

from which it follows that in equilibrium P must be 8. Substituting this value for P in either equation (1) or equation (2), we can easily calculate that the amount demanded and supplied in equilibrium must be 6.

Now comes the interesting part. The usual theory of equilibrium price which we get in elementary economics books tells us that if the actual market price happens to diverge from its equilibrium level of 8, the suppliers of the commodity will immediately react, in such a way that the price will very soon move back again to 8.

One way of illustrating what is supposed to happen is to imagine that for some reason or other the quantity of the commodity supplied falls temporarily below the equilibrium level of 6. Suppose, for example, that it falls to 5. Have a look at the graph. The demand curve shows us that consumers are prepared to pay a price of 9 per unit for a quantity of 5, and we assume that competition between consumers for the reduced supply will in fact raise the unit price to this higher level. The producers will now find that they are making higher than normal profits: the supply curve shows us that they would have been prepared to supply 5 units at a price of only $7\frac{1}{2}$ per unit, but they are in fact receiving 9 per unit. The demand price is higher than the supply price. So, the theory goes, the producers will immediately try to cash in on this happy state of affairs by increasing their output above 5 again. As they begin to do this, the unit price which consumers are prepared to pay will gradually fall below 9, and this process will go on until the equilibrium price and quantity are once again reached.

But suppose that the real-world situation is such that it is not plausible to assume that supply can be continuously adapted to demand in this way. Suppose, for example, that the commodity for which these are the demand and supply curves is rice, and that the suppliers are peasants in an under-developed country. Now in the case of a commodity like rice a long period necessarily elapses between sowing and harvesting—or, if you like, between the decision to produce a certain quantity and the actual putting of this quantity on the market. This means that the rise in the unit price to 9—caused in our example by a temporary fall in the quantity supplied to 5—will not affect the supply of rice *this year* at all. This year's supply is the result of *last year's* decisions (plus the effects of the weather, etc.), and is unalterable in the short period. Thus the price this year will remain at 9, and there will be no tendency for it to return to its equilibrium level.

But although the relatively high price of 9 cannot affect *this year's* supply, it may well affect *next year's*. Decisions as to how much to produce next year will have to be taken by the peasants this year, and they may well base these decisions very largely on this year's price. A relatively high price this year may make them optimistic, so that they plan to produce a relatively large amount next year.

If this is so, it may be reasonable to treat the amount supplied in any given year (call it year t, standing for $t$ime) not as a function of price in that year t—which is what we have so far in effect been doing—but rather as a function of price in the previous year, year $t-1$. Let us assume, then, that the supply curve in our graph now shows the functional relationship between this year's supply and last year's price. This means that in the place of the simple equation

$$S = 2P - 10$$

in which we in effect abstract from time, we now substitute a rather more realistic equation in which we 'date' the relevant quantities by attaching little tags 't' and '$t-1$' to them:

$$S_t = 2P_{t-1} - 10$$

In highbrow circles, this is called putting a lag into a model, a procedure which, in the present case, immediately raises all sorts of eye-popping possibilities, which I shall illustrate with the aid of Figure 6.2.

Let us start in a particular year which we shall call year 0. In that year, we shall assume, the quantity supplied has fallen below the equilibrium level of Q_E (= 6) to Q_0 (= 5), and as a result the price per unit has risen above the equilibrium level of P_E (= 8) to P_0 (= 9). The price, note carefully, starts in year 0 at *1 above* the equilibrium level. Now this price P_0 (= 9) will determine the supply in the next year, which we shall

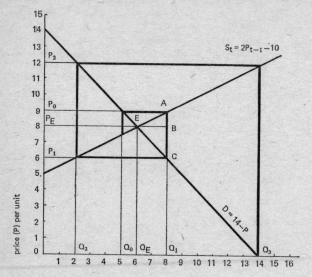

Figure 6·2

call year 1. This supply, as shown by the supply curve, will be Q_1 (= 8). But when Q_1 actually comes on to the market in year 1, it cannot in fact be sold at the unit price P_0 on the basis of which the producers' plans to supply Q_1 were arrived at. As shown by the demand curve, a supply as large as Q_1 can only be sold at a unit price of P_1 (= 6).

Thus the producers' expectations that the price in year 1 will remain the same as it was in year 0 are sadly disappointed. P_0 was *1 above* the equilibrium price, but P_1 is *2 below* the equilibrium price. Inevitably, if the slope of the demand curve is twice as great as the slope of the supply curve (as we are assuming in our example), P_1 must be twice as far below the equilibrium price as P_0 was above it. If the reader does not believe this let him have a look at the two triangles *EBA* and *EBC* on the graph. Since the slope of the demand curve is twice as great as the slope of the supply curve, the angle *BEC* must be twice as great as the angle *BEA*, and *BC* must therefore be twice as long as *BA*. Which proves the point, of course, since *BC* is the amount by which P_1 is below the equilibrium price and *BA* is the amount by which P_0 was above it.

Let us now put a little cap ⌃ over P_0 and P_1 to make these symbols mean the *deviations* of P_0 and P_1 from the equilibrium price. Then the result we have just reached can be expressed in more general form as follows:

$$\hat{P}_1 = \hat{P}_0 \left(\frac{\text{Slope of Demand Curve}}{\text{Slope of Supply Curve}} \right)$$

Since in our assumed case the ratio $\dfrac{\text{Slope of Demand Curve}}{\text{Slope of Supply Curve}}$ is equal to 2, the deviation of P_1 from the equilibrium price is twice as great as the deviation of P_0 from it.

Now carry this on into the next year, year 2. The price P_1 ($= 6$) will determine the quantity supplied in year 2, which the supply curve tells us will be Q_2 ($= 2$). But the demand curve tells us that this relatively small quantity Q_2 will in fact be sold in year 2, not at P_1 per unit, but at the much higher price P_2 ($= 12$). And the same logical reasoning as before tells us that P_2 will be twice as far above the equilibrium price as P_1 was below it. In other words,

$$\hat{P}_2 = \hat{P}_1 \left(\frac{\text{Slope of Demand Curve}}{\text{Slope of Supply Curve}} \right)$$

And since we already know that

$$\hat{P}_1 = \hat{P}_0 \left(\frac{\text{Slope of Demand Curve}}{\text{Slope of Supply Curve}} \right)$$

we can immediately deduce that

$$\hat{P}_2 = \hat{P}_0 \left(\frac{\text{Slope of Demand Curve}}{\text{Slope of Supply Curve}} \right)^2$$

In other words, we can deduce that the amount by which the price in year 2 deviates from the equilibrium price will be 2^2 times the original deviation of P_0 from the equilibrium price which started all the trouble.

This simple formula enables us to predict, on the basis of any given starting price, what the price will be after any stated number of years. In year 3, for example, we can deduce that

$$\hat{P}_3 = \hat{P}_0 \left(\frac{\text{Slope of Demand Curve}}{\text{Slope of Supply Curve}}\right)^3$$

In other words, we can deduce that the amount by which the price in year 3 deviates from the equilibrium price will be 2^3 times the original deviation of P_0 from the equilibrium price.[1] Thus the price P_3 itself will clearly be $8 - (2^3)(1)$—i.e., 0. With something of a shock, we realise that our imaginary economy has come face to face with some kind of awful crisis. A price of 0 will clearly elicit no supply at all in the next year. To use the technical jargon, the cobweb has exploded.

A good Zen exercise: imagine the sound of an exploding cobweb. It should not be any more difficult than solving a first-order difference equation, which (whether the reader is aware of it or not) is what we have just done.

Not *all* cobwebs explode, of course. Ours did for the simple reason that we assumed that the slope of the demand curve was greater than the slope of the supply curve—i.e., that the ratio $\frac{\text{Slope of Demand Curve}}{\text{Slope of Supply Curve}}$ worked out at greater than 1. And this need not necessarily be the case. Suppose, for example, that the slope of the demand curve is equal to the slope of the supply curve, as in Figure 6.3, so that the crucial ratio works out at equal to 1. In that case, $\hat{P}_1$ will obviously be equal to $\hat{P}_0$ (though opposite in sign), $\hat{P}_2$ will be equal to $\hat{P}_1$, and so *ad infinitum*. Clearly we will go round and round in an eternal oblong—never getting any further from the equilibrium price, it is true, but never getting any nearer to it either.

Take now a third possible case, in which the slope of the demand curve is less than the slope of the supply curve, as in Figure 6.4, so that the ratio works out at less than 1. We deduce immediately that in such a case $\hat{P}_1$ will be less than $\hat{P}_0$ (and opposite in sign), $\hat{P}_2$ will be less than $\hat{P}_1$, and so *ad infinitum*. Here we will go round and round in ever-decreasing

1. Generalising further, we can say that in *any* year t after year 0

$$\hat{P}_t = \hat{P}_0 \left(\frac{\text{Slope of Demand Curve}}{\text{Slope of Supply Curve}}\right)^t$$

concentric oblongs, finally reaching the equilibrium price once
again.

What use is this ingenious model? What can we do with it?
What we would like to be able to do with it, of course, is to
use it to predict what the price and output would be in, say,
three years' time, if we started with some price like P_0

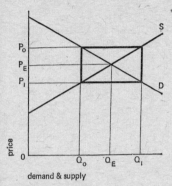

Figure 6·3

Theoretically, we *can* make such a prediction with the aid of
our simple formula, at any rate in the case of straight-line
demand and supply curves. But suppose the curves are *not*
straight lines? Obviously the task of prediction would then be
much more complicated. And even if we could get over that
one, it is very probable that during the relatively long time
period we are considering, the curves themselves would shift
around quite a lot, thus making the task of accurate prediction
virtually impossible.[2]

But the model may be able to help us, under certain circumstances, to predict at any rate that there is a danger of this
kind of oscillation occurring. If our studies suggest, for
example, that the slope of the demand curve (over the relevant
part of its length) is conspicuously greater than that of the
supply curve, *and* that the community is a relatively static one,
with incomes, tastes, techniques, etc., not changing much

2. Another point is that although in our cobweb model we have
introduced a lag into the supply equation, we have left demand un-
changed as a function of this year's price. If we introduce a lag into the
demand equation as well, things get very complicated indeed.

from one year to another, then the model at least enables us to predict that there is a danger of a potentially explosive cobweb-type oscillation occurring. If we then observe that large swings in prices and quantities demanded and supplied do in fact occur in successive years, it is a pretty fair bet that the type of mechanism our model has revealed is actually at work. And in such cases there are various remedial measures

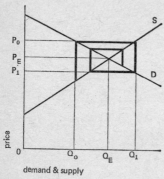

Figure 6·4

the Government may be able to take. It can encourage the diversification of crops, for example, showing people how to grow other crops and engage in other activities. It may be able to provide more and better information and forecasts concerning future prices, thus limiting the extent to which peasants have to look to this year's prices as the basis for their decisions about next year's output. Such uses for a model of this kind are by no means negligible.

The cobweb model is essentially an economic one. The second model which I want to describe in this chapter is much more sociological than economic. I first came across it, as a matter of fact, in the form of an intriguing half-obliterated diagram on the blackboard of a Sociology classroom at the University of Essex. The model which I reconstructed from the diagram—correctly, I hope—goes like this.

Consider the case of an underdeveloped country which needs foreign aid in order to develop, but which knows that foreign aid can only be obtained by the sacrifice of a certain amount of independence. Suppose that we measure amounts

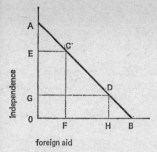

Figure 6·5

of foreign aid (in dollars, say) along the horizontal axis of a graph, and amounts of independence (in some unit of which we shall just have to imagine ourselves possessed) up the vertical axis (see Figure 6.5). Now if the country decided to do without any foreign aid at all, it would be able to enjoy a certain maximum amount of independence—*OA*, say. And if it decided to do without any independence at all, it would be able to enjoy a certain maximum amount of foreign aid—*OB*, say. The points *A* and *B* represent the two extremes at each end of a range of possible combinations of independence and foreign aid which are open to it—*OA* independence and zero foreign aid, and *OB* foreign aid and zero independence. In between these two extremes there are presumably other feasible combinations of independence and foreign aid—the point *C*, for example, representing a combination of *OE* independence and *OF* foreign aid, and the point *D*, representing *OG* independence and *OH* foreign aid. If we join up *A*, *B*, and all intermediate points like *C* and *D* we will get a line which we shall call the *line of feasible combinations*.[3]

Which of the large—possibly infinite—number of combinations on this line will the country in fact choose? This will depend upon its *pattern of preferences* as between independence and foreign aid. In our model, we draw a picture of

3. I have made it a *straight* line on the diagram purely for the sake of simplicity, thereby impliedly assuming that the 'price' of foreign aid—i.e., the extra amount of independence the country has to sacrifice for another dollar's worth of aid—remains the same however much or little aid the country is at the moment 'buying'. It would probably be more realistic to assume that the line of feasible combinations was in fact a curve, convex to the origin.

this pattern of preferences in the form of a family of what are usually called *indifference curves*, three of which—all absolutely imaginary—I have drawn in Figure 6.6. Each point on each curve represents a particular combination of independence and foreign aid: point *A* on curve 1, for example, represents a combination of *OG* independence and *OH* foreign aid. The curves are constructed in such a way that the country is *indifferent* between any of the combinations represented by the points on any individual curve, but prefers any point on a higher curve to any point on a lower curve.

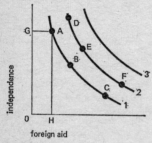

Figure 6·6

Thus if the country were offered a choice between combinations *A*, *B*, and *C* on curve 1, it would say: 'I don't care—they are all equally satisfactory.' If it were offered a choice between *D*, *E*, and *F* on curve 2 it would make the same reply. But if it were offered a choice between any point on curve 2—*D*, say—and any point on curve 1—*A*, say—it would reply: 'I prefer the point on curve 2'. Similarly, it prefers any point on curve 3 to any point on curve 2, and so *ad infinitum*.

The aim of the country, we assume, is to attain the highest indifference curve which is within its reach, *given* the practicable possibilities embodied in the line of feasible combinations. To find out what combination it will actually choose, all we have to do is to superimpose the line of feasible combinations on a diagram showing a number of the country's indifference curves (see Figure 6.7). The country *can* choose any combination on the line *AB*. It *will* choose the combination represented by the point *C* on indifference curve 3, since it will thereby attain the highest indifference curve within its reach. It *could* choose *F* or *G* if it wanted to, but if it did it would land up on an indifference curve lower than 3. It would *like* to choose some point on an even higher indifference curve like 4, but being confined to *AB* it cannot in fact do so. What it does, therefore, is to choose the point at which an indifference curve is just tangential to the line of feasible combinations.

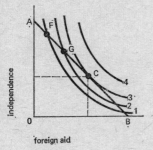

Figure 6.7

A little research resulted in the unearthing of another model in which the same technique is applied to a quite different problem.[4] In this model we assume that the management of an enterprise wants to maintain *authority* over its workers, but at the same time wants to *reduce conflict* with its workers (see Figure 6.8). Authority and conflict reduction are obviously two opposing organisational goals, like independence and foreign aid in the previous model. The enterprise can only have more industrial peace at the cost of less authority. Clearly we can deal with this problem in the same way as we dealt with the last one—by drawing a line of feasible combinations of authority and conflict reduction, superimposing a family of indifference curves upon it, and identifying the point at which an indifference curve is just tangential to the line.

The authors of this model go on to develop it in a very interesting way, revealing a number of facets of problems of this type which only come to the surface when this way of looking at them is adopted. One point which emerges, for example, is that a movement by the enterprise to a higher indifference curve on *its* diagram does not necessarily mean

4. See the last reference under 'Suggestions for Further Reading' at the end of this chapter.

that the workers are pushed to a lower indifference curve on *their* diagram. In other words, changes produced by industrial bargaining are not necessarily at the expense of one of the parties: it is at least possible under certain circumstances that both parties may gain.

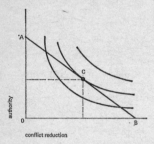

Figure 6·8

The authors feel that when sociologists really get down to measuring things, instead of just defining and conceptualising them, models of this sort may well be made 'operational'. And it is certainly true that considerable headway is being made, over the whole field of the social sciences, in the development of techniques for putting meaningful figures on certain things —like independence, for example—which at first sight do not seem to be measurable at all.

I think a little scepticism is in order here, however. Some models are much more likely to be made 'operational' than others—if only because the variables involved are more readily measurable and the relations between them more clear-cut and stable. And I rather doubt whether we shall ever be able to tell an underdeveloped country with any degree of exactitude how much independence and how much foreign aid it ought to choose if it wants to reach its highest possible indifference curve.

But a model does not necessarily stand or fall by its ability to serve as the foundation for quantitative predictions. Equally important in the case of some models is their ability to help us in the *organisation of our ideas* about the socio-economic processes concerned. They can often provide us with conceptual frameworks within which to make concrete analyses of these processes; they can help us to see similar forces operating in different situations; and they can suggest hypotheses to be tested. No one need apologise for experimenting with analytical models of the kind we have just been discussing.

Suggestions for further reading

On Models:
Economic Models, by E. F. BEACH (John Wiley & Sons, 1957)
Simple Models of Group Behavior, by O. J. BARTOS (Columbia University Press, 1967)

On the Cobweb Theorem:
Price Theory and Its Uses, by D. S. WATSON (Houghton Mifflin Co., 2nd Edn., 1968), chapter 13 and Mathematical Notes to Part Four

On Indifference Curve Analysis in Economics:
Price Theory and Its Uses, by D. S. WATSON, chapter 5 and Mathematical Notes to Part Two

On the Authority and Conflict Reduction Model:
'An Illustration of the Use of Analytical Theory in Sociology: The Application of the Economic Theory of Choice to Noneconomic Variables', by E. V. SCHNEIDER and S. KRUPP (*American Journal of Sociology*, May 1965)

Chapter 7

How to make profit all along the line

In which we are introduced to modern optimisation techniques, with special reference to marginal analysis and linear programming.

So far in this book, our main emphasis has been on the problems involved in sorting out, analysing, and above all quantifying the relations which exist between important socio-economic variables in the world we live in. Our main aim, if you like, has been to figure out the way in which men *do in actual fact* behave in their social and economic life, and to investigate some of the consequences of this behaviour.

Now we are going to change course a little. In the next four or five chapters we are going to be concerned not so much with the way in which men *do* behave in their social and economic life, but rather with the way in which they *ought* to behave. These two types of inquiry do not exist in separate water-tight compartments, of course: they are obviously interconnected. But the change of emphasis is sufficiently important to warrant my saying a few words about it before we begin.

Let us note right away that our inquiry into the way in which men ought to behave will *not* be concerned, at any rate directly, with the vexing problems of social ethics. All we are going to do is to assume that men want to fulfil a particular aim—let us call it provisionally the aim of *optimisation*, or making the best of it—and then show how they should act in order to fulfil this aim under various specified circumstances. We shall not be passing any moral judgements on the aim itself.

Let me give some examples of what I am going to mean by optimisation. A business firm, for instance, may be said to engage in an optimisation exercise if and when it tries to maximise its profits. To produce a good involves it in *costs*; when it sells the good it gets in *revenue*; and what it tries to do (or at any rate *may* try to do) is to produce just that quantity of the good, and to charge just that price for it, which maximises total profits—i.e., the difference between total revenue and total costs.

This is an example of a self-seeking optimisation exercise. But optimisation need not necessarily be self-seeking in this sense at all. Take a public enterprise—the Central Electricity Generating Board, for example. When the Board produces electricity, certain real *costs*, or sacrifices, are imposed on society, since the resources being used to produce the electricity cannot at the same time be used to produce any of the other things which society wants. And when the electricity is sold, the *benefits* which come from its use accrue to society. Presumably what the Board ought to do, as a public concern, is to act in such a way as to maximise the difference between total social benefits and total social costs. If it did not in fact act so as to do this, we would probably want to say that it was being inefficient, or wasteful, or acting irrationally, or something like that. Similarly an organisation like Oxfam ought to optimise, in the sense of maximising the difference between the total benefits accruing from its activities and the total costs which it incurs in carrying them out.

And individuals, as well as organisations, very often find themselves in situations where they want to optimise in some such sense as this. Sometimes it will be 'moral' for them to do so—as in the case of a housewife spending her weekly allowance for her family, and trying to allocate it among different goods in such a way as to get the most out of it. Sometimes it will be 'immoral' for them to do so—as in the case of a gambler playing a game of chance, and trying to work out the line of action which according to the laws of probability will maximise his gains (or minimise his losses).

Whether for good or for bad reasons, then, organisations and individuals very often wish to optimise, in the sense of acting so as to maximise the difference between benefit and cost, income and outgoings, or whatever you like to call it. The techniques of optimisation which we shall be considering tell us how to go about fulfilling this aim under various defined circumstances of greater or lesser complexity. In this chapter I shall begin by saying something about the way in which the so-called *marginal analysis* tackles the problem, and then go on to talk about the method of *linear programming*. In Chapter 8 I shall discuss *inventory control theory* and *queueing theory*; and in the three following chapters I shall deal with various aspects of the *theory of games*. All these are constituents of a new discipline—very much the product of our times—which is generally known as *Operations Research*.[1]

First, then, let us consider the method of *marginal analysis*. The general philosophy lying behind it is roughly as follows. Many human actions, particularly but not exclusively in the socio-economic sphere, involve (as we have just seen) both a cost and a benefit. To a consumer purchasing a good, for example, the cost involved is represented by the money he has to pay for it, and the benefit by the satisfaction he eventually receives from it. To a businessman producing a good, again, the cost involved is represented by the money he has to pay for the land, labour, and capital he uses in order to make the good, and the benefit by the revenue he gets in when he sells it.

In cases of this kind, we formulate the optimisation problem by asking *how many units* of the commodity the consumer or businessman concerned ought to purchase or produce, if his aim is to maximise the difference between total benefit and total cost. We imagine that he gradually increases the amount that he purchases or produces per period of time (per month, let us say), pausing after each unit increase to ask whether it is really worth his while to purchase or produce another unit; and we try to define the point at which he will *stop* increasing the amount in this way.

Take the businessman, for example. He is at the moment producing, let us say, 25 units of the good per month, and is wondering whether he ought to increase his monthly output to 26 units. If he does so his total monthly cost will go up by some calculable amount—£5, let us say. When he sells the additional unit on the market his total monthly sales revenue will also go up by some calculable amount. If this addition to total monthly sales revenue were greater than £5 (the addition to total monthly cost)—e.g., if it were £7—it would clearly be worth while for the businessman to produce 26 units per month instead of 25, since this would mean an addition of £2

1. A recent definition of Operations Research, taken from the first book noted in the 'Suggestions for Further Reading' at the end of this chapter, is as follows: 'Operations Research utilises the planned approach (scientific method) and an interdisciplinary team in order to represent complex functional relationships as mathematical models for the purpose of providing a quantitative basis for decision making and uncovering new problems for quantitative analysis.'

to his total monthly profits. So long as the addition to total monthly sales revenue through selling one more unit per month is greater than the addition to total monthly cost through producing it, the businessman will go on increasing his monthly output.

But he will not be able to go on doing this for ever. After a point, the production of each additional unit is likely to involve him in a greater and greater amount of extra cost; and it may well be that after a point he will have to reduce the unit price of his good in order to be able to sell a greater quantity of it. So the gap between the addition to total revenue associated with the sale of one more unit (*marginal revenue* in the jargon) and the addition to total cost associated with its production (*marginal cost*) will gradually become narrower and narrower. When output has been increased to the point where this gap has become zero—i.e., to the point at which marginal revenue is just equal to marginal cost—the businessman ought to stop increasing his output. He has now exhausted all the profit-making possibilities implicit in the situation which confronts him. If he increased his output further, into the region where marginal revenue is less than marginal cost, his total profits would be reduced. Total profits are maximised, then, when output is such that marginal revenue equals marginal cost.

Let us draw a diagram (Figure 7.1) to illustrate the kind of situation we are analysing. In this diagram we measure total monthly revenue in pounds (TR) and total monthly cost in pounds (TC) up the vertical axis, and the number of units of monthly output (x) along the horizontal axis. Let us assume that the price which the businessman gets for his product is £2 per unit, and that this unit price does not alter as his monthly output and sales increase. This means that for any given value of x the total monthly revenue will be £$2x$; and the functional relationship between monthly output and total monthly revenue will come out on our graph as a straight line starting at the origin and going up from left to right with a slope of 2, as shown.

We must now postulate some kind of functional relationship between monthly output and total monthly cost. This relationship is unlikely to be a straight-line one, and in the real world it is often quite complex. To simplify the problem as much as possible without being *too* unrealistic, let us assume that the relationship is such that total monthly cost in pounds is always one-quarter of the square of the number of units of monthly output—i.e., in terms of our shorthand, that

$$TC = \tfrac{1}{4}x^2$$

When we graph this relationship, it comes out as the curve in the diagram, which starts at the origin and goes up from left to right with a slope which gets greater and greater as monthly output increases.

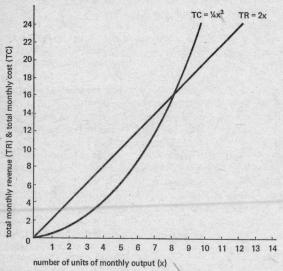

Figure 7·1

The businessman, we assume, wants to produce that output at which the difference between *TR* and *TC* is maximised—i.e., that output at which the vertical distance between the *TR* line and the *TC* curve is a maximum. Given the data which we are assuming is at his disposal, the businessman can pick on this profit-maximising output very simply by taking a ruler and measuring the vertical distances between the line and the curve at various outputs, starting at zero output and gradually working his way along. In the early stages he will find that the vertical distance between the line and the curve increases as output increases. The reason is that in these early stages, when output is increased by one unit TC increases by less than TR, since the *slope* of the TC curve at any given output is less than the *slope* of the TR line at that output. Or, to put the same thing in another way, in these early stages *marginal cost* is less than *marginal revenue*.[2] This will go on being the case until the businessman gets to an output of 4. Beyond the output of 4, he will find that the vertical distance between TR and TC, representing total profits, begins to *de*crease as output is increased. The reason is that in the range of output above 4, when output is increased by one unit TC increases by *more* than TR, since the slope of the TC curve at any given output has become *greater* than the slope of the TR line at that output. In other words, marginal cost has become greater than marginal revenue. The businessman, therefore, should stop at the output 4, at which the slopes of the TC curve and the TR line are equal—i.e., at which marginal cost is equal to marginal revenue, and total profits are maximised.

The businessman could have arrived at this solution without drawing a graph at all, provided that he knew what the actual functional relationships between the variables were. The profit-maximising output must be that output at which marginal cost is equal to marginal revenue. All that the businessman needs to do, therefore, is to work out what marginal cost and marginal revenue are at each possible output, and then pick on that output at which they are equal.

So far as marginal revenue (MR) is concerned, there is not much difficulty in working it out. For each additional unit produced, TR goes up by £2, the price at which the additional unit is sold, so that whatever the output MR always stays the same, at £2. It is not quite so easy, however, to put a figure on marginal cost (MC), because this clearly does *not* stay the same, but changes as output changes.

The problem we are faced with here is this: given that

2. The slope of the TR line at any given level of output measures the amount by which TR will increase if output is increased above that level by one unit—i.e., it measures marginal revenue. Similarly, the slope of the TC curve at any given level of output measures the amount by which TC will increase if output is increased above that level by one unit—i.e., it measures marginal cost—*provided, in this case, that the unit increase is very small in relation to the number of units previously being produced*. This rather tricky point is explained more fully in the Mathematical Appendix, section 10, pp. 221–4.

$TC = \frac{1}{4}x^2$ (where $x =$ the number of units of monthly output), can we derive from this an equation which shows, for any given value of x, by how much TC will go up when x increases above that value by one (small) unit? In other words, given that we know the functional relationship which exists between *total* cost and x, can we derive from this the functional relationship which exists between *marginal* cost and x?

This is really what the *calculus* is all about. One of the most important things the calculus can do is to provide us with a general formula which enables us to solve problems of this type. If, it says,[3] an independent variable x and a dependent variable y are functionally related in such a way that $y = ax^n$, where a and n are constants, then the amount by which y will go up when x increases by one (very small) unit will be nax^{n-1}. Suppose, for example, that the functional relationship between an independent variable x and a dependent variable y is such that $y = 3x^4$, so that $a = 3$ and $n = 4$. In that case, the amount by which y will go up when x increases by one (very small) unit will be $4 . 3 . x^{4-1}$, i.e., $12x^3$.

All right—in our profit maximisation problem the independent variable is output (x) and the dependent variable is TC. We know that $TC = \frac{1}{4}x^2$, so that $a = \frac{1}{4}$ and $n = 2$. The general formula provided by the calculus therefore tells us that the amount by which TC will go up when x increases by one (small) unit—i.e., MC—will be $2 . \frac{1}{4} . x^{2-1}$, which works out at $\frac{1}{2}x$.

It is now all over bar the shouting. We know[4] that $MR = 2$, and we have just calculated that $MC = \frac{1}{2}x$. The level of output (x) at which profits are maximised will be that at which $MR = MC$—i.e., that at which $2 = \frac{1}{2}x$. This naturally means that $x = 4$—i.e., that the profit-maximising monthly output is 4 units.

Having now shown how we can get the right answer to this kind of optimisation problem either by pure logic, or by geometry, or by the use of the calculus, we must now go on to

3. For a proof of this proposition, see the Mathematical Appendix, section 11, pp. 224–7.

4. We could also have used the same general formula, if we had wanted to, in order to work out MR. We know that $TR = 2x$ (which can be written $2x^1$), so that $a = 2$ and $n = 1$. Thus according to the formula MR will be $1 . 2 . x^{1-1}$, i.e., $2x^0$; and since $x^0 = 1$ we once again get the right answer, 2.

point out the limitations of marginal analysis. This method is fine when the conditions are nice and straightforward, as we have assumed them to be in our problem—where the business-man is producing only one commodity, where the relevant cost and revenue curves are smooth and continuous and do not have any sudden kinks or breaks in them, and where it is physically possible for the businessman to produce *any* of the levels of output which we measure along the base line of our graph. But if any of these conditions do not in fact apply, then we simply cannot use the marginal method at all.

Suppose, for example, that the businessman can produce *two* different products and has to decide on some kind of combination of them. Suppose, too, that his capacity to produce them is by no means unlimited, but is *constrained* by, say, a limited supply of conveyor belts and a limited supply of labour. The marginal method will then be completely useless, and some other technique of optimisation will have to be adopted. It is to deal with cases like this that the techniques of *mathematical programming* have been developed. I shall be dealing here only with the most simple of these—the method of *linear programming*[5].

A manufacturer turns out two types of radios—a standard model which we shall call 1, and a luxury model which we shall call 2. These two models can be sold at a profit of 20 pence and 30 pence each respectively. So if the manufacturer produces a quantity r_1 of standard radios and a quantity r_2 of luxury radios every day, he will make a total daily profit of $20r_1 + 30r_2$ pence. His problem, we shall assume, is to choose that particular combination of the two models which maxi-mises his total profit, given that he is subject to the two following constraints upon the range of production possi-bilities open to him:

(*a*) *A conveyor belt constraint.* Production takes place on two separate conveyor belts, one for each model. The capacity of these belts is limited. The capacity limit in the case of model 1 is 7 per day. Thus the daily output of model 1 radios must be either less than or equal to 7—i.e.,

$$r_1 \leqslant 7$$

5. The example which follows is taken from *Operations Research and Quantitative Economics*, by H. Theil, J. C. G. Boot, and T. Kloek (McGraw-Hill Book Co., 1965).

The corresponding capacity limit in the case of model 2 is 5 per day, so that

$$r_2 \leqslant 5$$

(b) *A labour supply constraint*. There are only 12 workers employed in the factory, so that a total of 12 man-days is all that is available on any given day. It requires 1 man-day to make a standard (model 1) radio, and 2 man-days to make a luxury (model 2) radio. If r_1 of model 1 and r_2 of model 2 are produced per day, this will take a total of $r_1 + 2r_2$ man-days. So we have the following additional constraint:

$$r_1 + 2r_2 \leqslant 12$$

To illustrate the method of solution prescribed by the technique of linear programming, let us draw a picture of the situation with which the manufacturer is confronted. We start by constructing a graph in which the quantity of model 1 radios produced per day (r_1) is measured along the horizontal axis, and the quantity of model 2 radios produced per day (r_2) is measured up the vertical axis. On this graph, we set out to depict all the combinations of models 1 and 2 which it would be *physically possible* for the manufacturer to produce, given the two constraints. Let us deal with the constraints in isolation from one another in the first instance, and then proceed to put them together so as to get the complete picture.

First, consider the conveyor belt constraint. If both conveyor belts were used full tilt, the manufacturer could produce 7 of model 1 and 5 of model 2 each day. This combination is represented by the point *A* in Figure 7.2. He could not produce more than this of either model, but he could if he wished produce *less* than this of either or both of them. In terms of the graph, what this means is that he could produce any combination represented by a point on or within the rectangle *OBAC*, but that he could not produce any combination represented by a point outside it.

Second, consider the labour supply constraint ($r_1 + 2r_2 \leqslant 12$). What combinations of models 1 and 2 could the manufacturer produce without exceeding this limit? Well, one possible combination would be 6 of model 2 and 0 of model 1, which he could produce if he used all the available labour to produce model 2. This combination is represented by the

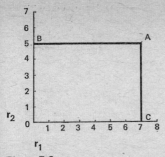

Figure 7·2

point *D* in Figure 7.3. Another possible combination would be 12 of model 1 and 0 of model 2, which he could produce if he used all the available labour to produce model 1. This combination is represented by the point *E* on the graph. In between these two extremes, he could produce many other

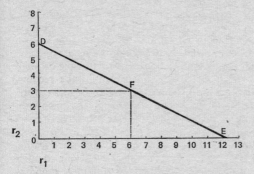

Figure 7·3

combinations, such as, for example, 6 of model 1 and 3 of model 2, a combination represented by the point *F* on the graph. If we take all such possible combinations and join up the relevant points we will get a straight line, as in the graph.[6]

6. The fact that we get a straight line when we do this, rather than a curve, should not surprise the reader if he has managed to get this far. What we have done, in effect, is to graph the function $r_1 + 2r_2 = 12$ (or, if you like, $r_2 = 6 - \frac{1}{2}r_1$), and we surely know by now that the graph of a functional relationship of this type always comes out as a straight line.

In the face of the labour supply constraint, then—which it will be remembered we are at the moment considering in isolation—the manufacturer could clearly produce any combination represented by a point on or within the triangle *ODE*, but he could not produce any combination represented by a point outside it.

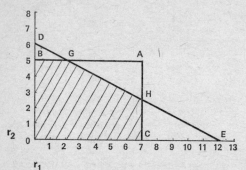

Figure 7·4

Now let us put the two diagrams together (Figure 7.4), and consider the situation when both the constraints are operating at once. When that is the position the only feasible combinations are those which lie both on or within the rectangle *OBAC and* on or within the triangle *ODE*. In other words, the only feasible combinations are those which lie on or within the area common to the rectangle and the triangle, i.e., the shaded pentagon *OBGHC*.

We now have a picture of what combinations are *feasible*. Our aim, however, is to ascertain which particular combination among all those that are feasible is the most *profitable*, and to answer this question we have to bring into the picture the manufacturer's assumed profit function, viz.

$$\text{Total Profit} = 20r_1 + 30r_2$$

The way in which we bring it in is like this. We begin by asking what combinations of 1 and 2 would yield a total daily profit of some given (arbitrary) amount—say 60 pence. We ask, in other words, what values of r_1 and r_2 would satisfy the equation

$$20r_1 + 30r_2 = 60$$

Well, one such combination would be 3 of r_1 and 0 of r_2, represented by the point J in Figure 7.5. Another would be 2 of r_2 and 0 of r_1, represented by the point K. And any other combination represented by a point on the straight line between K and J would also yield a total profit of 60 pence.

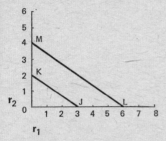

Figure 7·5

Now let us ask what combinations of 1 and 2 would yield a total daily profit of some other given (arbitrary) amount—say, £1.20. One such combination would be 6 of r_1 and 0 of r_2, represented by the point L; another would be 4 of r_2 and 0 of r_1, represented by the point M; and any other combination on the straight line between M and L would also yield a total profit of £1.20. Thus as the assumed amount of total profit is increased, the straight line representing the range of combinations which will yield this profit moves outward from the origin, but without altering in slope.

We are now ready for the final step. In Figure 7.6 I have redrawn the pentagon of feasible combinations $OBGHC$ from Figure 7.4, and superimposed upon it four total profit lines—the lines KJ and ML (representing profits of 60 pence and £1.20 respectively) which we have just been discussing; a new line NP which represents a profit of £2.15, and which just touches the pentagon at the point H; and another new line QR which represents a profit of £3.

Now the manufacturer would like very much to get a daily profit as high as £3. In other words, he would like to be able to produce a combination represented by one of the points on the line QR. But he could not in fact do this, because the two constraints confine him to combinations on or within the pentagon $OBGHC$. He could get a daily profit of 60 pence by producing a combination represented by one of the points on the line *KJ*. But he would not in fact do this, because he could get a profit twice as great as this by producing a combination represented by one of the points on the higher profit line *ML*. *Or, still better, he could get a profit of £2·15 by producing the combination represented by the point H on the pentagon, which is also (although only just) a point on the line NP.*

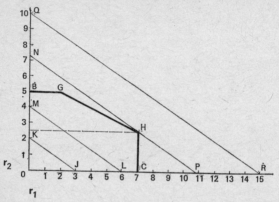

Figure 7·6

Clearly this is the best that the manufacturer could do: to get a profit any higher than £2.15 he would have to produce a combination outside the feasible region *OBGHC*, which by definition would be impossible.

(If at this stage the reader is getting a strong sense of *déjà vu*, he should refer back to pp.82–5 and note the interesting family resemblance between this linear programming model and the second of our two 'underdeveloped models' in the last chapter.)

We can read off from the diagram what the optimum profit-maximising combination represented by the point *H* actually is. It consists of 7 of model 1 and $2\frac{1}{2}$ of model 2. And we could have got the same result, in this relatively simple case, by a piece of elementary algebra. We know that the number of model 1 sets in the combination represented by the point *H* is 7.[7] We also know that this combination just satisfies the labour supply constraint, so that $r_1 + 2r_2 = 12$. Sub-

7. The reader should refer back to Figure 7.4 if this is not clear.

stituting the value of 7 for r_1 in this equation, it immediately emerges that $r_2 = 2\frac{1}{2}$.

In real life, of course, the optimisation problems faced by manufacturers are much more complex than the one we have taken as our example. There may well be many more than two products to be considered, and many more than two constraints; and it will not then be possible to draw a picture of the situation on a relatively simple two-dimensional graph. But even in the more complicated cases, the experts tell us, it remains true that the optimum combination will always be *on* the 'boundary' and not within it, and that in most cases the solution will be a 'corner point' like B, G, H, C, or O in our diagram.[8]

This gives us a clue—although necessarily a rather indefinite one—to the nature of the mathematical method which is normally employed to solve these more complex problems. Essentially, what any method of solution has to do is to identify all the combinations at 'corner points' analogous to B, G, H, C, and O in our diagram; to substitute these in the profit equation (or in the analogous equation which fulfils a similar role); and to select that combination which yields the best possible outcome. Fortunately a very fast short-cut method of hitting on the optimum combination, known as the simplex method, has been developed. This is incredibly ingenious, but since it would take me too far out of my way to discuss it here I shall have to leave the reader to admire it for himself in one or other of the numerous books which deal with it.[9]

8. I have put 'boundary' and 'corner point' in quotation marks to indicate that these words mean something different in the two-dimensional case we have just considered from what they would mean in a multi-dimensional case.

9. The basic principles of the simplex technique are well described in *Operations Research and Quantitative Economics*, by Theil, Boot, and Kloek.

Suggestions for further reading

On Operations Research:

Decision Making Through Operations Research, by R. J. THIERAUF and R. A. GROSSE (John Wiley & Sons, 1970)

A Guide to Operational Research, by ERIC DUCKWORTH (Methuen & Co., 2nd Edn., 1965)

On Marginal Analysis and the Calculus:

Economic Theory and Operations Analysis, by W. J. BAUMOL (Prentice-Hall, 2nd Edn., 1965), chapters 3 and 4

On Linear Programming:

The Science of Decision-making, by ARNOLD KAUFMANN (Weidenfeld and Nicolson, 1968), chapters 2 and 3

Operations Research and Quantitative Economics, by H. THEIL, J. C. G. BOOT, and T. KLOEK (McGraw-Hill Book Co., 1965), chapter 1

Chapter 8

How to mind your peas and queues

In which we pursue further our study of Operations Research, building an 'inventory control model' for a retail grocery store and a 'queueing model' for a petrol filling station.

The manager of a large retail grocery store comes to us with a problem that is worrying him. The total annual demand by his customers for tinned peas of a particular brand is 12,000 tins. This demand manifests itself at a rate per unit of time which (for the sake of simplicity) we assume to be constant and known in advance to the manager. In order to be able to meet the demand at the times when it manifests itself the manager must keep a certain number of tins of peas in stock, and when his stock runs out he must order a new supply from the producers. The problem is that of the number of tins which he ought to order from the producers at one time, assuming that he wants to minimise his total operating costs.

One *possible* solution would be to order the whole 12,000 tins at the beginning of the year—on 1st January, say—and to let this stock gradually run down (at the constant rate which it will be remembered we are assuming) until it reaches zero on 31st December. The average number of tins in stock per unit of time, known as the average inventory, would then be 6,000 tins—i.e., one-half of the order size. This is illustrated in Figure 8.1, where the downward-sloping line traces out the gradual decline in the quantity of tins held in stock as the year proceeds from its beginning to its end.

If he adopted this procedure, the manager would have only one order to give to the producers each year, so that his total annual *ordering costs* would be very low. *Ordering costs* are the costs associated, for example, with issuing the purchase order, following it up if necessary, taking receipt of the goods, putting them into stock, and settling up with the producers. Clearly his total annual ordering costs will be greater, the greater is the *number* of orders he places during the year, so that with only one order they will be relatively low.

But his total annual *carrying costs* will then be relatively high. *Carrying costs* are the costs associated, for example, with the use of warehouse space to store goods, and with the locking-up of money capital in the goods so stored.[1] Clearly his total annual carrying costs will be greater, the greater is the *size* of the order or orders he places, so that with a single order of 12,000 tins they will be relatively high.

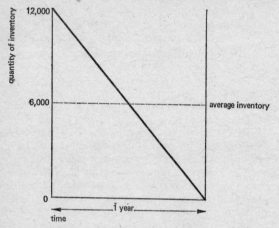

Figure 8·1

A large order size, then, may mean low total annual ordering costs, but at the same time it means high total annual carrying costs. And, conversely, a small order size may mean low total annual carrying costs, but at the same time it means high total annual ordering costs. Suppose, for example, that the manager changed from one order of 12,000 tins per year to six orders of 2,000 tins. His total annual carrying costs would certainly then go down, since his average inventory would be reduced from 6,000 to 1,000 tins (see Figure 8.2). But at the same time, since he would now be giving six times as many orders per year as he did before, his total annual

1. At bottom, the costs involved here are what economists call 'opportunity costs'—e.g., the rent which *could have been earned* for the warehouse space if it had been used for some purpose other than that of storing the tins of peas, and the interest or profit which *could have been earned* on the money capital if it had not been locked up in these stocks.

ordering costs would be six times as great.[2] The problem for
the manager is to find the most profitable possible compromise between the two extremes—i.e., to hit upon that particular order size which makes the *sum* of total annual carrying
costs and total annual ordering costs as small as it can possibly be under the given circumstances. How can we help him
to find this optimum order size?

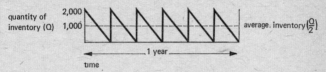

Figure 8·2

Let us feel our way towards a general solution of the problem on the basis of the particular case we have just been
considering. Our grocery manager's annual demand for
tinned peas, we have assumed, is 12,000 tins. Let us now
assume further that each of these tins costs him 10 new pence;
that total annual carrying costs are always 20% of the money
value of the average inventory carried during the year; and
that ordering costs are always £7.50 per order. Given these
figures, we can fairly easily work out the total annual carrying-
plus-ordering costs which will be associated with each of a
number of possible order sizes.

This is done in Table 8.1. In column 1, under the heading
'Order Size' (which we symbolize by the letter Q), we list a
number of possible order sizes (i.e., values of Q) ranging
from 12,000 down to 1,000. In column 2 we list the number of
orders per year which would be necessary, in the case of each
of the order sizes listed in column 1, to enable the firm to
meet the total annual demand of 12,000 tins. If the size of the
order were 12,000 only one order per year would be necessary;
if it were 6,000 two would be necessary; and so on. If we call
the total annual demand D, the number of orders per year will
be D/Q.

In column 3 we give the money value of the average inven-

2. This is on the assumption, which we are again making purely for
the sake of simplicity, that the cost of giving an order remains the same
whatever the size of the order or the frequency with which orders are
made.

Table 8.1

1	2	3	4	5	6
Order Size (Q)	No. of Orders Placed Per Year $\left(\frac{D}{Q}\right)$	Money Value of Average Inventory $\left[\frac{Q}{2}(C)\right]$	Total Annual Carrying Costs $\left[\frac{Q}{2}(CI)\right]$	Total Annual Ordering Costs $\left[\frac{D}{Q}(S)\right]$	Total Annual Carrying-plus-Ordering Costs $\left[\frac{Q}{2}(CI) + \frac{D}{Q}(S)\right]$
12,000	1	£600	£120	£7·50	£127·50
6,000	2	£300	£60	£15	£75
4,000	3	£200	£40	£22·50	£62·50
3,000	4	£150	£30	£30	£60
2,000	6	£100	£20	£45	£65
1,500	8	£75	£15	£60	£75
1,200	10	£60	£12	£75	£87
1,000	12	£50	£10	£90	£100

tory which will be associated with each of the order sizes in column 1. The average inventory in *physical* terms will in each case be one-half of the order size (i.e., $Q/2$). In *money* terms it will be this physical number of tins multiplied by the assumed cost per tin of 10 pence. If we call the cost per tin C, the money value of the average inventory will be $\frac{Q}{2}(C)$.

In column 4 we give the total annual carrying costs, which we have assumed are always 20% of the money value of the average inventory. If we call this percentage I, the total annual carrying costs will be $\frac{Q}{2}(CI)$.

In column 5 we give the total annual ordering costs, which are simply the numbers of orders per year in column 2 multiplied by the assumed ordering costs of £7.50 per order. If we call ordering costs per order S, total annual ordering costs will be $\frac{D}{Q}(S)$. Finally, in column 6 we add up the figures in columns 4 and 5 to obtain the total annual carrying-plus-ordering costs which will be associated with the various order sizes in column 1. In terms of our symbols, these total annual carrying-plus-ordering costs will be $\frac{Q}{2}(CI) + \frac{D}{Q}(S)$.

The way in which the quantities in columns 4, 5, and 6 behave as the order size increases can be seen more clearly if we graph the three functions concerned. This is done in Figure 8.3. The function relating total annual carrying costs to order size, it will be seen, is linear, proceeding upwards from left to right at a constant slope. The function relating total annual ordering costs to order size, on the other hand, is non-linear, proceeding downwards from left to right at an ever-decreasing slope. In the early stages, at the left-hand side of the diagram, the total annual ordering costs function slopes downwards more steeply than the total annual carrying costs function slopes upwards, which indicates that at this stage the decrease in total annual ordering costs associated with a (small) increase in order size is greater than the increase in total annual carrying costs associated with it. And this in turn logically implies that total annual carrying-plus-ordering costs must be declining—which they indeed are at this stage, as can be seen both from the graph (where the total annual carrying-plus-ordering costs function is the vertical sum of the other two) and from the table. But there eventually comes a point at which the downward slope of the total annual ordering costs function (which is constantly decreasing) comes into equality with the upward slope of the total annual carrying costs function, thereafter falling below it. It logically

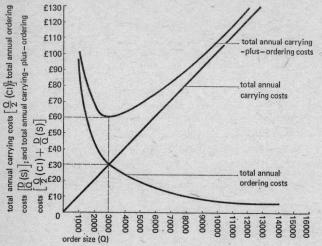

Figure 8·3

follows that at this point total annual carrying-plus-ordering costs must reach their minimum level, thereafter beginning to rise again.

In the particular case we are considering, as can be seen both from the graph and from the table, this crucial point is apparently reached when Q assumes a value of 3,000, which is associated with total annual carrying-plus-ordering costs of £60.[3] Now the interesting thing here is that at this optimum order size of 3,000 *total annual carrying costs are equal to total annual ordering costs*. In other words, the optimum order

3. I say 'apparently' because we have specifically examined only a fairly limited range of possible order sizes: for all we know at the moment, it is at least conceivable that an order size of, say, 2,900 or 3,100 might be associated with total annual carrying-plus-ordering costs of less than £60. As a matter of fact, however, an order size of 3,000 *is* the optimum one in the present case. I have selected my figures very carefully!

size seems to be defined by the point of intersection of the total annual carrying costs curve and the total annual ordering costs curve. We shall now show that this is not merely an accident peculiar to the present case, but a necessary feature of the optimum solution in *all* cases of the general type we are considering.

If the sum of total annual carrying costs $\left[\dfrac{Q}{2}(CI)\right]$ and total annual ordering costs $\left[\dfrac{D}{Q}(S)\right]$ is to be a minimum, we know that the value of Q must be that at which the upward slope of the $\dfrac{Q}{2}(CI)$ function is equal to the downward slope of the $\dfrac{D}{Q}(S)$ function. We also know from the last chapter that the slope of a function, for any given value of the independent variable, can be derived from the function by the application of a general formula provided for us by the calculus.[4]

Now $\dfrac{Q}{2}(CI)$ can be written as $\left(\dfrac{CI}{2}\right)Q^1$, so that for the purposes of the application of our formula $a = \dfrac{CI}{2}$ and $n = 1$. The slope of the total annual carrying costs function, for any given value of Q, is therefore $1 \cdot \dfrac{CI}{2} \cdot Q^{1-1}$, which works out at $\dfrac{CI}{2}$. And $\dfrac{D}{Q}(S)$ can be written as $(DS)Q^{-1}$, so that in this case $a = DS$ and $n = -1$. The slope of the total annual ordering costs function,[5] for any given value of Q, is therefore $-1 \cdot DS \cdot Q^{-1-1}$, which works out at $-(DS)Q^{-2}$, or $-\dfrac{DS}{Q^2}$.

If total annual carrying-plus-ordering costs are to be a minimum, therefore, the value of Q must be that at which the upward (positive) slope $CI/2$ is equal to the downward

4. To repeat: if $y = ax^n$, where y is a dependent variable, x is an independent variable, and a and n are constants, then the amount by which the value of y will go up when x increases by one (very small) unit (i.e., the slope of the function) will be nax^{n-1}.

5. Readers who are puzzled by the fact that the slope of the first function comes out as a positive quantity whereas that of the second comes out as a negative one should consult the Mathematical Appendix, section 10, p. 219.

(negative) slope $-DS/Q^2$. When two quantities are equal to one another but of opposite sign they add up to zero, so that the condition for a minimum can be stated as:

$$\frac{CI}{2} + \left(-\frac{DS}{Q^2}\right) = 0$$

That is, $\dfrac{CI}{2} = \dfrac{DS}{Q^2}$

If we now multiply each side of this equation by Q, the condition becomes

$$\frac{CI}{2}(Q) = \frac{DS}{Q}$$

That is, $\dfrac{Q}{2}(CI) = \dfrac{D}{Q}(S)$

In other words, it is immaterial whether we express the condition for a minimum in terms of the equality of the slopes of the functions *or in terms of the equality of total annual carrying costs and total annual ordering costs*. If the value of Q is such that one of these equalities is brought about, then the other will be automatically brought about as well. The fact that in our example the optimum order size was defined by the point of intersection of the total annual carrying costs curve and the total annual ordering costs curve was *not* an accident.

Our final task is to derive from the condition for a minimum a general formula for practical application in cases of this type. This is just a matter of simple manipulation:

If $\dfrac{CI}{2} = \dfrac{DS}{Q^2}$

then $Q^2 = \dfrac{2DS}{CI}$

and $Q = \sqrt{\dfrac{2DS}{CI}}$

This is the famous 'square root formula', which was first put forward in 1915 and which constitutes the essence of the inventory model we have been building. Applying it to our grocery store case, we can work out the optimum value of Q

immediately, without the necessity of constructing any tables or drawing any graphs at all:

$$Q = \sqrt{\frac{2DS}{CI}} = \sqrt{\frac{2 \times 12{,}000 \times 7{\cdot}50}{0{\cdot}10 \times 1/5}}$$

$$= \sqrt{9{,}000{,}000} = 3{,}000$$

Our model, as we have developed it, is of course based on a number of simplifying assumptions—e.g., that the demand for the good manifests itself at a rate per unit of time which is constant and known in advance—and if any of these assumptions are not in fact true of a particular real-world situation which we are examining, the model naturally has to be extended and refined. But even as it stands, in its relatively crude form, it can tell us quite a lot that we might not otherwise appreciate.

For example, we might think—as some businessmen apparently do—that if the annual demand doubled, the order size should also be doubled. But a glance at our formula shows us that this would be quite wrong: if D doubled, Q would in effect be multiplied not by two but by the square root of two, which is a very different matter.

In addition, to take another example, the model can give us two pieces of good advice if we are unable to put *exact* values on the variables D, S, C, and I. First, it can tell us that there is no need to worry *too* much about this. It can be seen from the table on p. 106 (and also proved from the square root formula as a universal result)[6] that an over- or under-estimation of Q, unless it is a *very* serious one, is not going to make all that much difference to the total annual carrying-plus-ordering costs. Starting from the optimum order size of 3,000, we see that an over-estimation of $33\frac{1}{3}\%$ will increase these costs by only $4\frac{1}{6}\%$; an over-estimation of 100%, by only 25%; an under-estimation of $33\frac{1}{3}\%$, by $8\frac{1}{3}\%$; and an under-estimation of 50%, by 25%. Second, a comparison of these results of an over-estimation and an under-estimation of Q suggests that the latter is likely to have a worse effect on costs than the former, other things being equal. The model tells us, therefore, that when in doubt we ought to err on the generous side in fixing the level of Q.

6. See *Operations Research and Quantitative Economics*, by Theil, Boot, and Kloek, pp. 190–192.

Let us now turn to the second of the two optimisation techniques to be dealt with in this chapter—that designed to solve the so-called 'queueing problem'.

Queues, like the poor, are always with us. Motorists have to wait at traffic lights; people wanting to get their hair cut have to wait at the hairdresser's; machines which go wrong in a factory have to wait to be repaired. And waiting almost always *costs* something. The person waiting for the traffic lights to change, or for the hairdresser to work his way through the queue, *could* have been doing something else with the time—earning money, for example, or improving his mind. And the operatives in the factory who are standing around waiting for their machines to be repaired *could* have been working, and earning profits for their employer.

Waiting could of course be avoided. Traffic lights could be done away with by constructing over- and under-passes. The managers of hairdresser's shops could employ more hairdressers. The factory owner could enlarge his repair shops. But to do these things would obviously be expensive. Waiting may cost something, but so does doing away with waiting.

So here, once again, we have one of those problems upon which Operations Research thrives—how to steer an optimum course between the Scylla of waiting costs and the Charybdis of waiting-avoidance costs. This problem presents itself in practice in many different ways, of widely differing degrees of complexity.

The manager of a small petrol filling station, employing only one attendant, comes along to us with a problem. He has not been in business very long, he tells us, and although he is doing fairly well he is getting a bit worried by the length of time his customers seem to be having to wait for service. It is not that the attendant is inefficient: the *average* time he takes to deal with a customer is only just over three minutes, although naturally in any individual case it may be more or less than this. Nor are his customers arriving all that frequently: the *average* time between arrivals is just under four minutes, although naturally the time between any two individual arrivals may be either greater or less than this. But because the rates of arrival and service per unit of time are not uniform, but *random*, queues quite frequently form and customers then have to wait for service.

The manager has been told by friends that if customers find

that they have to wait on the average more than 1 minute for service, they are likely to change to rival filling stations where the waiting time is less. The manager wants to know, therefore, what the average waiting time at his filling station (over a longish period) is likely to be. And if it turns out to be near the crucial level of 1 minute, he also wants to know whether he should employ a second attendant.

At first sight it might seem that the only way of dealing with this problem would be to go down to the filling station and take full records of waiting times over quite a long period—which would, of course, be an irksome and costly business. Fortunately, however, it is possible to do the job quite quickly without stirring out of one's office—particularly if one has a computer handy.

All we really need to know is the frequency with which the times between arrivals, and the times of service, fall into different ranges of time. The manager may be able to tell us, for example, that taking one day with another the time between arrivals in 20% of the cases falls in the 2–3 minute range; in 40% in the 3–4 minute range; in 30% in the 4–5 minute range; and in the remaining 10% in the 5–6 minute range. He may also be able to tell us that, again taking one day with another, the time of service in 40% of the cases falls in the 2–3 minute range; in 50% in the 3–4 minute range; and in the remaining 10% in the 4–5 minute range. With this information, we can draw two diagrams (Figures 8.4 and 8.5) showing the *probability* with which the time between arrivals and the time of service will respectively fall within the ranges concerned. The probabilities are measured on a scale running from 0 to 1: an event which will happen in 20% of the cases is assigned a probability of 0·2; in 40% a probability of 0·4; and so on.

On the basis of this information alone, and with the aid of some counters and a hat, we can *simulate* the operation of the filling station, arrival by arrival and service by service, for as long a period as we wish. The idea is that we proceed from one car to the next, assigning a randomly-chosen time between arrivals and a randomly-chosen time of service to each successive case, *taking care that the probability of any particular time being chosen is that shown in the diagrams.*

The easiest way to do the job is this. Take ten counters and write the figure '2' on two of them, '3' on four of them, '4' on three of them, and '5' on the remaining one. These are the

counters we shall use in selecting the successive lengths of
time between arrivals for the simulation model we are building. If we put them into a hat, shake them up, and draw them
out one at a time (with replacement), it is clear that (*a*) our
choice will always be 'random' in the sense that we shall never
know what number we are going to draw next; but that (*b*) if

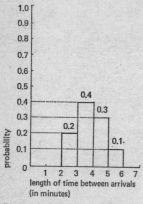

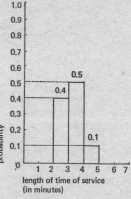

Figure 8·4   *Figure 8·5*

we draw a sufficiently large number of counters we shall find
that 2's have been drawn in 20% of the cases, 3's in 40%, 4's in
30%, and 5's in 10%. Let us take the number on each successive counter we draw, then, as indicating the successive
times between arrivals as the day proceeds.[7]

Now we take another ten counters, and write the figure '2'
on four of them, '3' on five of them, and '4' on the remaining
one. These are the counters we shall use in selecting the
successive lengths of time of service for our simulation model.
If we put them in a hat and draw them out as just described,
we can safely use the number on each successive counter we
draw as indicating the successive lengths of time of service as
the day proceeds.

7. The reader will note that in adopting this procedure we are in effect
using the number at the *lower end* of each range to represent the range.
It would be more rational, perhaps, in the absence of any further
information, to use $2\frac{1}{2}$, $3\frac{1}{2}$, $4\frac{1}{2}$, and $5\frac{1}{2}$ instead of 2, 3, 4, and 5. We use
the latter for the sake of simplicity, in order to avoid having to deal in
fractions of a minute.

We now prepare a table like Table 8.2, with headings as shown.[8] The working day, we shall assume, starts at 8.00 a.m. Drawing a counter from our first set we get, say, a 3, and put this down in the first column of the table. The first car, then, arrives at 8.03 a.m., and we put this time down in the second column. The service of this car can begin immediately, at 8.03, so we put this time down in the third column. The attendant has waited 3 minutes, but the customer has not had to wait at all, so we put 3 and 0 in the sixth and seventh columns respectively.

We now remove the first set of counters from the hat and replace them with the second set,[9] drawing one of these out to indicate the service time in respect of the first car. We get, say, a 2. The service of the first car, then, ends at 8.05, and we put 2 and 8.05 down in the fourth and fifth columns respectively. There are now figures in all the columns except the eighth.

Now we go through the process again. Drawing a counter from the first set, we get, say, a 4, which means that there is an interval of 4 minutes between the arrival of the first car and that of the second. We can therefore start the second line of figures by putting 4 in column 1 and 8.07 in column 2. Since the service of the first car ended at 8.05, the second car does not have to wait in line, so that we can now put a zero at the end of the first line of figures in column 8. The service of the second car can begin immediately at 8.07, so we enter this figure in column 3. The attendant has had to wait 2 minutes, but the customer has not had to wait at all, so we enter 2 in column 6 and 0 in column 7. We now draw another counter from the second set to find the service time in respect of the second arrival. We get, say, a 4, and can then fill in columns 4 and 5. And so we go on, for as long as we think necessary in order that accidents should be ironed out and an accurate overall picture obtained.

The results of an actual experiment, which I carried out as I was writing this, are recorded in Table 8.2. I continued with the exercise until the filling station had dealt with 40 cars, over a period of $2\frac{1}{4}$ hours. There is not a sufficient quantity of data

8. This is based on a simulation worksheet in *Decision Making Through Operations Research*, by R. J. Thierauf and R. A. Grosse, p. 457.
9. If the reader carries out this experiment for himself—and it is a very worth-while exercise indeed—he will soon find that two hats are better than one!

1	2	3	4
Time Till Next Arrival, in Mins. (Random Number)	Arrival Time	Service Begins	Time of Service in Mins. (Random Numb
3	8.03	8.03	2
4	8.07	8.07	4
2	8.09	8.11	2
3	8.12	8.13	3
3	8.15	8.16	2
4	8.19	8.19	2
3	8.22	8.22	2
2	8.24	8.24	3
3	8.27	8.27	2
5	8.32	8.32	3
4	8.36	8.36	3
2	8.38	8.39	3
3	8.41	8.42	4
4	8.45	8.46	4
4	8.49	8.50	3
3	8.52	8.53	3
4	8.56	8.56	2
4	9.00	9.00	4
5	9.05	9.05	2
5	9.10	9.10	2
4	9.14	9.14	4
3	9.17	9.18	4
2	9.19	9.22	2
4	9.23	9.24	3
4	9.27	9.27	3
2	9.29	9.30	3
2	9.31	9.33	2
5	9.36	9.36	2
3	9.39	9.39	3
4	9.43	9.43	3
2	9.45	9.46	3
3	9.48	9.49	3
2	9.50	9.52	3
3	9.53	9.55	2
2	9.55	9.57	2
4	9.59	9.59	2
2	10.01	10.01	2
5	10.06	10.06	2
3	10.09	10.09	3
3	10.12	10.12	3

5	6	7	8
Service Ends	Waiting Time of Attendant	Waiting Time of Customer	Length of Line
8.05	3	0	0
8.11	2	0	1
8.13	0	2	1
8.16	0	1	1
8.18	0	1	0
8.21	1	0	0
8.24	1	0	0
8.27	0	0	0
8.29	0	0	0
8.35	3	0	0
8.39	1	0	1
8.42	0	1	1
8.46	0	1	1
8.50	0	1	1
8.53	0	1	1
8.56	0	1	0
8.58	0	0	0
9.04	2	0	0
9.07	1	0	0
9.12	3	0	0
9.18	2	0	1
9.22	0	1	1
9.24	0	3	1
9.27	0	1	0
9.30	0	0	1
9.33	0	1	1
9.35	0	2	0
9.38	1	0	0
9.42	1	0	0
9.46	1	0	1
9.49	0	1	1
9.52	0	1	1
9.55	0	2	1
9.57	0	2	1
9.59	0	2	0
10.01	0	0	0
10.03	0	0	0
10.08	3	0	0
10.12	1	0	0
10.15	0	0	–
		25	

in this table to enable us to draw any really firm conclusion, of course: many weeks of simulated data—which could be provided in a very short time by a computer—would be necessary before one could have any real faith in the result. Nevertheless, it is possible, on the basis of the table, to give a provisional answer to the manager's first question. The filling station has dealt with 40 cars, and the total waiting time of customers has been 25 minutes, making an average waiting time (per customer) of $\frac{25}{40}$, i.e., 0·625 minutes. This is well below the crucial average figure of 1 which the manager was told would result in the transfer of clients' custom to rival firms, so we are probably justified in assuring him that he need not worry about this.

Under these circumstances, there is of course no need for the manager to contemplate hiring another attendant. But suppose that the average waiting time had worked out appreciably higher, and that the manager was able to put a figure on the amount and value of the custom he was likely to lose as a result of this. We could then clearly carry out another exercise of the same kind, comparing total costs and receipts with one attendant and a lot of waiting time, and costs and receipts with, say, two attendants and little or no waiting time. Then again, if the conditions of the problem were expected to change—e.g., if the manager anticipated some given increase or decrease in the average time between arrivals —we could use the model to tell him how this would affect the average waiting time.

The model as we have developed it, like the other model which we considered earlier in the chapter, is based on certain simplifying assumptions—e.g., that the probability distributions set out in the diagrams are applicable in each hour of the day, and that the attendant does not allow pretty lady drivers to jump the queue. The model naturally requires extension and refinement in cases where these assumptions do not hold. Nevertheless, even as it stands it can throw a great deal of light on the essential nature of the queueing problem and the component factors determining its make-up. In addition, in the form in which I have presented it here, it provides a good illustration of the use in Operations Research of the so-called 'Monte Carlo method', whereby a process of random selection of numbers is employed in order to generate data for use in a simulation model.

Suggestions for further reading

On Inventory Control Models:
>   *Decision Making Through Operations Research*, by R. J. THIERAUF and R. A. GROSSE (John Wiley & Sons, 1970), chapter 7
>   *Operations Research and Quantitative Economics*, by H. THEIL, J. C. G. BOOT, and T. KLOEK (McGraw-Hill Book Co., 1965), chapter 11

On Queueing Models:
>   *Decision Making through Operations Research*, by R. J. THIERAUF and R. A. GROSSE, chapter 14
>   *Operations Research and Quantitative Economics*, by H. THEIL, J. C. G. BOOT, and T. KLOEK, chapter 9

On the Monte Carlo Method:
>   *The Science of Decision-making*, by ARNOLD KAUFMANN (Weidenfeld and Nicolson, 1968), chapter 4

Chapter 9

How to beat Professor Meek and Professor Moriarty

In which the author plays a finger game with the reader, thereby introducing him to the theory of games and a literary application of it.

Warning: Do not look at page 125 until you are asked to.

In a minute or two I am going to invite you to play a game with me. The game is a very simple version of an old 'finger game' called Morra. The moves I am going to make in the game are set out on page 125, and if you knew what they were going to be you could beat me easily and the whole point of playing the game would be lost. So please do heed the warning above!

Before I introduce the game to you and tell you the rules, I ought to give you some idea of what all this is about. The point is that there are many situations in social, economic, and political life in which individuals or groups find that their basic interests are diametrically opposed. We then say the parties are in a conflict situation, or obliged to act under conditions of extreme social conflict, or something like that.

So common are these conflict situations, and so important, that a great deal of modern social and economic theory is concerned with the way in which a rational individual or group ought to behave when involved in a situation of this kind. The newest and most exciting development in this field is the so-called Theory of Games, originally worked out by von Neumann and Morgenstern in 1947.

The basic idea lying behind this theory is a very simple one. Many of these conflict situations, when you look into them, seem to bear a strong family resemblance to situations which arise in certain simple parlour games like poker, or matching pennies, or Morra. In these games a player has to choose one out of a number of alternative lines of action, and the net outcome of his move— the final payoff, if you like—depends not only on what he does but also on the move which his opponent simultaneously makes. The Theory of Games assumes in effect that if we can work out the principles of rational behaviour in simple games of this kind, we may be able to extend and apply these principles to much more serious and complex fields such as military strategy, or economic competition, or class war.

To our game, then. The idea is that we both in effect simultaneously show either one finger or two. If we both show the same number of fingers (whether one or two), I win 2p from you. If I show one finger and you show two, you win 3p from me. If I show two fingers and you show one, you win 1p from me.

The following payoff table, in which the plus and minus signs represent gains and losses *from my point of view*, summarises the situation:

Reader

		one finger	two fingers
	one finger	+2p.	−3p.
Prof. Meek	two fingers	−1p.	+2p.

The potential gains which I may make add up to 4p, and the potential gains which you may make also add up to 4p. So the game is a perfectly fair one.[1]

Do not look yet, but on page 125 the moves I am going to make in the game are set out. There are five adjacent columns, headed 'First Set', 'Second Set', etc., each of which contains 40 figures. Each figure is either a 1, meaning that I show one finger, or a 2, meaning that I show two fingers. The order in which the 1's and the 2's appear reflects a cunning strategy which I have adopted, and which naturally I do not propose to reveal to you until the game is over.

Before we start, you will need two pieces of card or opaque paper about the size of a page of this book. When I tell you to do so, put these over page 125 as in the illustration overleaf. One piece is to be used, as you see, to cover up all the figures in columns 2 to 5. The other is to be used to uncover one by one the successive figures in column 1. You will also need to

1. Or is it? More about this later.

have a pencil and paper handy so that you can keep the score as you go along.

Before you uncover the first figure in column 1, show either one or two fingers yourself. Then uncover the first figure, which represents the number of fingers which I wish simultaneously to show. Work out your gain or loss in accordance

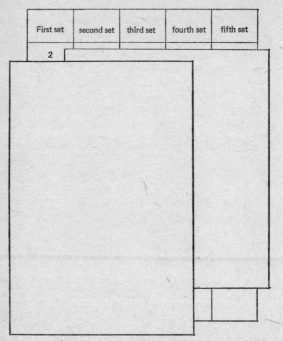

First set	second set	third set	fourth set	fifth set
2				

with the payoff table above, and make a careful note of it. Then repeat the performance, gradually going down the column and trying as hard as you can to detect my strategy and to adopt an appropriate counter-strategy. After 40 games you will have reached the end of the first column—but not, I hope, of your endurance. Tot up the scores and see how much you have won or lost.

If you feel like it, you can then go ahead and play a second 'set' of 40 games—and a third, fourth, and fifth if you like—with the aid of the figures in the remaining four columns. The more games you play the more likely you are to learn the secret, and with any luck your gains may increase—or your losses diminish—as you proceed from one 'set' to another. I warn you, however, that I shall be going all out to win!

If you are sure you understand the instructions, turn now to page 125, cover up the figures, and let us start playing.

• • • • •

Did you win, or did I? The chances are that I did; but since you just might have been lucky I shall not bet on it. What I can say, with some confidence, is that if the results of all games played by all readers of this book could be collected and added up, I would most certainly win. I could also predict, with equal confidence, the amount of my winnings: on average, I would win ½p per game. Let me explain why I am so sure about this.

In pitting my wits against yours, I naturally assumed that you were an intelligent person, and therefore started with three basic principles:

1. Obviously I had to play some kind of *mixture* of 1's and 2's. If I had played 1 all the time, you would very soon have cottoned on and started playing 2 all the time, thereby winning 3p in every game. Similarly, if I had played 2 all the time, you would very soon have started playing 1 all the time, thereby winning 1p in every game. So clearly I had to play some kind of mixture.

2. Whatever mixture I decided upon, I had to call the numbers in an irregular and not a regular sequence. Suppose, for example, that I had decided to play 1 and 2 in the ratio 4:5—i.e., to play 1 four times for every five times I played 2. Obviously it would have been very silly, given this decision, for me to play four 1's, then five 2's, then four 1's, then five 2's, and so on. You, as an intelligent person, would very soon have seen what I was doing, and started chiming in at the appropriate moment with a matching sequence of four 2's, five 1's, four 2's, five 1's, and so on, thereby winning either 3p or 1p in every game. So, having decided on the overall ratio in which I was going to play 1's and 2's, I obviously had to jumble the numbers up in such a way that you could not predict what was going to come next.

3. In deciding on the way in which the numbers ought to be jumbled up, I had to avoid the temptation to try 'psychologi-

cal' tricks—like, for example, starting with a regular sequence such as 1, 2, 1, 2, 1, 2 and then suddenly altering it. In assuming you to be an intelligent person, I naturally had to assume that if I tried anything like that you would eventually see through it and turn it to your own advantage, as you very easily could. So the jumbling process had to be left entirely to chance.

Now came the crucial question—in what overall ratio should I in fact play the two numbers? Here I felt I had to assume that you, as an intelligent person, would sooner or later discover what my strategy was and work out an appropriate counter-strategy designed to minimise my gains (or maximise my losses). So my job was to find that strategy which would maximise my gains (or minimise my losses) *in the face of your best possible counter-strategy*.

Let us try a few possible strategies which I might have adopted, and see what would have happened if I had in fact adopted them. Suppose, first, that I had played 1 and 2 in the ratio 9:1—i.e., that in each 'set' of 40 games I had played 36 1's and four 2's. Your best response, as you would probably very soon have discovered, would have been to play 2 every time, thereby winning 3p per game in nine games out of ten. This would have represented an average gain for you (and an average loss for me) of $2\frac{1}{2}$p per game.[2]

Suppose, second, that I had played 1 and 2 in a ratio near the other extreme end of the scale—1:9, say. This would have meant that in each 'set' of 40 games I would have played four 1's and 36 2's. In that case, your best response would have been to play 1 every time, thereby winning 1p per game in nine games out of ten. This would have represented an average gain for you (and an average loss for me) of $\frac{7}{10}$p per game.[3]

Suppose, third, that I had played 1 and 2 in a ratio somewhere in between these two extremes—1:1, say. Your best answer then—although it would probably have taken you a bit longer to work this out—would once again have been to play 2 every time, thereby winning 3p in half the games and losing 2p in the other half. This would have represented an

2. In 36 games I play 2 and you play 2, so that in these games you win a total of 108p. In 4 games I play 1 and you play 2, so that in these games I win a total of 8p. Your net gains (and my net losses) overall are thus 100p, i.e., an average of $2\frac{1}{2}$p per game.

3. Work it out for yourself as in the last footnote.

First Set	Second Set	Third Set	Fourth Set	Fifth Set
2	1	2	1	1
1	1	1	2	2
1	2	2	1	1
2	1	2	1	2
2	2	2	2	1
1	2	1	2	1
1	2	2	1	2
2	2	2	1	2
2	1	1	2	2
1	2	2	1	2
2	2	2	2	2
2	2	2	2	2
2	2	1	2	2
2	2	2	2	2
2	2	1	2	1
1	2	1	2	2
1	1	1	2	1
2	2	1	1	1
2	2	2	1	2
2	2	2	2	1
1	2	2	1	2
1	2	1	1	2
2	1	2	1	2
1	1	1	2	1
2	1	2	2	2
2	1	1	2	2
2	1	2	2	2
2	1	2	2	1
2	1	2	1	2
1	1	2	2	1
2	2	2	2	1
2	1	1	2	1
2	2	2	2	2
1	2	1	1	2
2	1	2	2	2
1	2	2	2	1
1	2	1	2	1
1	2	2	1	2
2	2	1	2	2
2	2	2	1	2

average gain for you (and an average loss for me) of $\frac{1}{2}$p per game.[4]

Let us put down the results so far in the form of a table:

My Strategy	Your Best Counter-Strategy	My Average Loss per Game
(1) Play 1's and 2's in a 9:1 ratio	Play 2's every time	$2\frac{1}{2}$p
(2) Play 1's and 2's in a 1:9 ratio	Play 1's every time	$\frac{7}{10}$p
(3) Play 1's and 2's in a 1:1 ratio	Play 2's every time	$\frac{1}{2}$p

If I were limited to these three strategies, then, I would obviously choose the third, because that would be the strategy which minimised my average losses in the face of your best possible counter-strategy. But, of course, I am *not* in fact limited to these three strategies; and the question immediately arises as to whether I could do better—possibly even making a gain instead of a loss—by adopting some *other* strategy in between the two extremes.

This is where the Theory of Games comes in. In a simple two-person game of this kind, where my loss is your gain and vice versa, I can work out my optimum strategy by an arithmetical procedure which is so absurdly easy—and so apparently arbitrary—that I am convinced that some sinister cantrip must be involved. Using the payoff matrix as your basis, you carry out the two arithmetical steps illustrated in the diagram opposite, finishing up with the figure 3 opposite my 'One Finger' row and the figure 5 opposite my 'Two Fingers' row. And this is the right answer! My optimum strategy, given that you will adopt your best possible counter-strategy, is to play 1's and 2's in a 3:5 ratio.

This is the strategy which I in fact adopted in the game we have just played. To get the figures which I used, I took 40 counters, marked 15 of them with a 1 and the other 25 with a 2, put them all into a hat, mixed them up thoroughly, and drew them out at random one at a time. The first time I did this they came out in the order of the figures in the 'First Set'

4. Any other strategy on your part would have resulted in an expected gain of less than $\frac{1}{2}$p per game, given a sufficiently large number of games to allow lucky and unlucky shots to cancel one another out. If you do not believe this, try it and see.

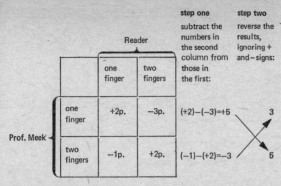

column; the second time in the order of those in the 'Second Set' column; and so on.

If I play 1's and 2's in a 3:5 ratio, then, what will your best possible counter-strategy be? And given that you adopt this counter-strategy, what will my average gains or losses per game be? The answer to the first question, oddly enough, is that *any* counter-strategy will be the best: if I play my optimum strategy (3:5 in the present case), the result will be exactly the same whatever counter-strategy you adopt.[5] And the answer to the second question is that if we play a very large number of games, so that bits of bad luck are cancelled out by bits of good luck, I will make an average gain of $\frac{1}{8}$p per game —i.e., a total gain of 5p per 'set' of 40 games. Take four illustrations.

1. I play 1's and 2's in a 3:5 ratio, and you play 1's all the time. Then:

	You Play	Result
In 15 games I play 1	1	+30p
In 25 games I play 2	1	−25p
	My Net Gain =	+5p

2. I play 1's and 2's in a 3:5 ratio, and you play 1's and 2's in a 4:1 ratio. Then:

	You Play	Result
In 15 games·I play 1		
In $\frac{4}{5}$ (= 12) you play	1	+24p
In $\frac{1}{5}$ (= 3) you play	2	−9p

5. This is not necessarily true for more complicated games.

In 25 games I play 2
    In $\frac{4}{5}$ (= 20) you play   1   −20p
    In $\frac{1}{5}$ (= 5) you play   2   +10p

                            My Net Gain = + 5p

3. I play 1's and 2's in a 3:5 ratio, and you play 1's and 2's in a 2:3 ratio. Then:

	You Play	Result
In 15 games I play 1		
In $\frac{2}{5}$ (= 6) you play	1	+12p
In $\frac{3}{5}$ (= 9) you play	2	−27p
In 25 games I play 2		
In $\frac{2}{5}$ (= 10) you play	1	−10p
In $\frac{3}{5}$ (= 15) you play	2	+30p
My Net Gain =		+ 5p

4. I play 1's and 2's in a 3:5 ratio, and you play 2's all the time. Then:

	You Play	Result
In 15 games I play 1	2	−45p
In 25 games I play 2	2	+50p
My Net Gain =		+ 5p

Thus if I play my optimum strategy of 3:5, I will in the long run make an average gain of $\frac{1}{8}$p per game in the face of your best possible counter-strategy (which in this case happens to be *any* strategy). And *it can be proved* that I cannot possibly do better than this with any other strategy, given that you adopt your best possible counter-strategy. Certainly I could not do better—and would in fact do conspicuously worse—if I adopted a strategy of 9:1, 1:9, or 1:1, as a glance back at the table on p. 126 will show.

The moral of all this, so far as the game we have just played is concerned, is pretty clear. My best course was to do as I did, playing 1's and 2's in a 3:5 ratio but in random order. Given that I was doing this, your best counter-strategy was *any* strategy. You could have played 1:0, or 1:1, or 3:4, or 0:1, or anything else you wished, but you would not have been able to push my average expected gains down below $\frac{1}{5}$p per game. You could always of course have shut your eyes, picked the numbers arbitrarily, and kept your fingers crossed—and you might possibly have done better. But on the other hand you might possibly have done much worse. Probably the most sensible thing would have been for you to play some strategy that stopped you from getting too bored, and then to sit back and accept the inevitable. The man is obviously a villain: he has loaded the game in his own favour.

But—and here I want to lead on to a very important point— the strategy you adopted would *not* have been immaterial if you had been playing with me face to face, so that I had the opportunity to follow your successive moves and detect *your* strategy in the same way as you had the opportunity to detect mine. *In that case, everything which I have spoken of above as applying to me and to my strategy would also have applied to you and to your strategy. You too would have had to discover that strategy which minimised your losses (or maximised your gains) in the face of your opponent's best possible counter-strategy.* And once again the Theory of Games could have told you how to find it. The exercise is essentially the same as before, except that we now do the operation as it were downwards instead of sideways:

Reader

	one finger	two fingers
Prof. Meek one finger	+2p.	−3p.
two fingers	−1p.	+2p.

step one
subtract the numbers in the second row from those in the first:

$(+2)-(-1)$ $(-3)-(+2)$
$=+3$ $=-5$

step two
reverse the results, ignoring + and − signs:

5   3

Your optimum strategy, if you were playing with me face to face, would be to play 1's and 2's in a 5:3 ratio.[6] If you adopted this strategy you would still lose an average of $\frac{1}{8}$p per game, but you would nevertheless be doing as well as you possibly could, since if you adopted any strategy other than 5:3 I could find a counter-strategy which would push your losses above $\frac{1}{8}$p per game.

So if we were playing face to face, the rational thing would be for me to play 3:5 and for you to play 5:3, with me winning and you losing an average of $\frac{1}{8}$p per game. Once we had got ourselves into that position we would be in a kind of equilibrium. I would not want to move away from 3:5, because if I did so you could adopt a counter-strategy which would push my gains below $\frac{1}{8}$p per game. And you would not want to move away from 5:3, because if you did so I could adopt a counter-strategy which would push your losses above $\frac{1}{8}$p per game. Each of us would be adopting the strategy which maximised his gains or minimised his losses in the face of his opponent's best possible counter-strategy.[7]

That is all I want to say at the moment about the general ideas lying behind the Theory of Games. Let us now turn to the first of a number of picturesque applications of these ideas.

In Conan Doyle's last Sherlock Holmes story, *The Final Problem*—the one in which the wicked Professor Moriarty eventually disposes of Holmes by pushing him into the Reichenbach falls—an interesting incident occurs. Moriarty is pursuing Holmes with the intention of murdering him.

---

6. The symmetry of these results—3:5 for me and 5:3 for you—is a pure accident.

7. The rules described above for finding the optimum strategies do not apply to games with payoffs like those in the accompanying matrix, where the figure which is the larger of the two row minima (the $+2$p in the top left-hand box) is also the smaller of the two column maxima. In the technical jargon of the Theory of Games, this is a game with a 'saddle point', and the players ought to adopt and stick to the alter-

	1	2
1	+2p.	+3p.
2	+1p.	−1p.

natives which as it were intersect at this saddle point. I should play 1 all the time and you should also play 1 all the time. If we were doing this, neither of us would have any incentive to change. While I was playing 1, you would lose less by playing 1 than by playing 2; and while you were playing 1, I would gain more by playing 1 than by playing 2. It is only when the game does *not* have a saddle point that the concept of mixed strategies and the method for working out optimum strategies described in the text are applicable.

Holmes gets into a train at Victoria with the aim of travelling to Dover, whence he hopes to escape to the Continent. The train is scheduled to stop for a few minutes at Canterbury on the way to Dover. Moriarty just misses the train at London, so he hires a special train which thunders down the track in the wake of the Continental express. So two great questions arise. First, where should Holmes get off, Canterbury or Dover? And second, where should Moriarty get off, Canterbury or Dover?

Clearly this is a problem upon which the Theory of Games might be able to throw some light. We can easily construct a payoff matrix of the same type as the one we used in our finger game, but it is a bit more difficult to put actual figures into the four boxes. If Moriarty and Holmes both get off at Canterbury, Moriarty will make a murderous assault on Holmes, and although (as Holmes says in the story) this is 'a game at which two may play', there is no doubt that if it happens Holmes will be seriously injured, if not killed. So let us put a large payoff of, say, $+100$ for Moriarty in the upper left-hand box. And since the same thing will happen if they both get off at Dover, let us put $+100$ in the lower right-hand box as well.

Holmes

	canter-bury	dover
canter-bury	$+100$	-50
dover	0	$+100$

Prof. Moriarty

If Moriarty gets off at Dover and Holmes gets off at Canterbury, this is really a stalemate, since Holmes will still be in England and Moriarty can turn back on his tracks and pursue him again. So perhaps we should put zero in the lower left-hand box. If Moriarty gets off at Canterbury and Holmes gets off at Dover, this represents something of a victory for Holmes since he escapes to the Continent, at any rate temporarily. So let us put -50 in the upper right-hand box.

How should this game be played? It does not have a saddle point;[8] mixed strategies are therefore involved; and according to the methods prescribed by the Theory of Games the appropriate strategies are that Moriarty should play Canterbury and Dover in the ratio 2:3, and Holmes should play Canterbury and Dover in the ratio 3:2.

But what does playing the two alternatives in a prescribed ratio actually *mean* in the present context? It had an unequivocal meaning in our finger game for the simple reason that we played the game a large number of times. And in the problem we are now considering it would presumably have a similar sort of meaning to this if we assumed that Holmes found himself faced with the same kind of situation very frequently in the course of his professional career—as he might conceivably have done if he had escaped from the Reichenbach falls and Moriarty had stayed on the warpath. Holmes could then plausibly play a 3:2 strategy by getting off at Canterbury three times for every twice he got off at Dover. Or, a little less fancifully, suppose that Holmes was one of a large number of detectives employed by Scotland Yard who were constantly getting into the same kind of trouble with Moriarty. In that case, the mortality of detectives could presumably be minimised by instructing 60% of them to get off at Canterbury and the remaining 40% to get off at Dover. This is pretty bizarre, perhaps, but there is an interesting and very serious analogy here with problems which arise in the field of military strategy, to which I shall return in the next chapter.

Given that the Holmes–Moriarty game is in fact to be played only once, however, what interpretation should be placed on the strategy prescriptions? To the authors of the Theory of Games this raised no problem whatever: *in fact the basic theory was originally developed with explicit reference to one play of a game*, and I have cheated a bit in introducing the theory to you in a many-game context. Holmes and Moriarty, the theory suggests, should both make their choice by using some kind of random device which in Holmes's case will make the odds 3:2 in favour of Canterbury and which in Moriarty's case will make the odds 3:2 in favour of Dover. Holmes might do it, for example, by taking five counters, putting 'Canterbury' on three of them and 'Dover' on the other two, and picking one of them out of Dr. Watson's hat.

8. See footnote 7 on p. 130 above.

And Moriarty might adopt a similar kind of procedure, putting 'Dover' on three of his counters and 'Canterbury' on the other two.

This all sounds very odd indeed, but there is some interesting reasoning behind it. A player in a game of this sort, it is argued, does not know what his opponent is going to do, and since the game is played only once he has no opportunity of finding out. Therefore, since anything may happen, the player might as well assume, in the interests of security, that the worst will happen—i.e., that the action which his opponent takes will turn out to be the most effective possible counter to his own. That is the first point. The second is that a player ought to act in such a way as to maximise his 'expected' payoff (in the mathematical sense), in the face of his opponent's most effective possible response. The best short definition of 'expected' payoff is long-term average payoff. So what this second point means, in effect, is that the player in a single game ought to take that action which, if it were taken in every play of a long series of games, would maximise his average gain per game, in the face of his opponent's best possible response.

That may sound complicated, but the game we played together a few minutes ago can help to explain it. If I had been playing with you face to face, I could have proceeded by putting three '1' counters and five '2' counters in a hat, picking one out on each play of the game, and showing that number of fingers. If I had done this in every play of a long series of games, the overall result would have been the same as it in fact was—I would have played 1's and 2's in a 3:5 ratio, thereby maximising my gains (at $\frac{1}{8}$p per game) in the face of your best possible response. So if I do this counters-and-hat operation in a *single* game, I shall be maximising my 'expected' payoff in the mathematical sense, in the face of my opponent's best possible response.

That is the reasoning behind the curious behaviour prescribed for Moriarty and Holmes. Personally I find it rather unconvincing. To maximise 'expected' payoff by the use of a random device may make good sense if one is playing a long series of games and can therefore actually *realise* the 'expected' payoff; but it does not seem to me to make good sense if one is playing only a single game and therefore *cannot* realise it. I am also worried about the notion that each player in the single game ought to assume that the worst will happen. This seems implicitly to counsel a degree of caution and security-mindedness which may not be 'right' at all—at any rate for some games and some players.[9]

Would it really be rational for Moriarty to choose between Canterbury and Dover in the way prescribed? By doing so he would, it is true, be maximising his 'expected' payoff, in the face of Holmes's most effective response. If Moriarty made the odds 3:2 in favour of Dover, his 'expected' payoff would be $+40$,[10] and it is certainly true that if he made the odds anything else his 'expected' payoff could be pushed below this if Holmes made his most effective response. But what does this matter if there is only a single game to be played? The value of $+40$, after all, does not appear in any of the boxes in the matrix. What will in fact happen is that Moriarty will choose either Canterbury or Dover. He is rather more likely to choose Dover, since there are three 'Dover' counters in his hat and only two 'Canterbury' counters, but it is at least a distinct possibility that he will pick out a 'Canterbury' one. If he does this, and Holmes happens to choose Dover, Moriarty's actual payoff will be -50. Surely if we are going to counsel security-mindedness, we ought to advise Moriarty simply to choose Dover, since the worst thing that could then happen from his point of view would be an actual payoff of 0. Which is better, after all—a mathematical 'expectation' of $+40$ which is nevertheless consistent with an actual payoff of -50, or the certainty of having an actual payoff of at least 0?[11]

One difficulty about advising Moriarty to do this is that the payoffs in this game are such that one cannot very usefully

9. It is true that in the game which I played with you I also assumed, in a way, that the worst would happen. But this was only because I had very good grounds for supposing that it actually would. It was merely realistic, and not unduly cautious, to assume that you would sooner or later discover any strategy which I adopted and take the appropriate counter-measures. To assume *in a single game* that the worst will happen is a different matter entirely.

10. If Holmes got off at Canterbury, the 'expected' payoff for Moriarty would be $\frac{2}{5}(+100) + \frac{3}{5}(0) = +40$. If Holmes got off at Dover, the 'expected' payoff for Moriarty would be $\frac{2}{5}(-50) + \frac{3}{5}(100) = +40$. If Holmes chose between Canterbury and Dover at 1:1 odds, the 'expected' payoff for Moriarty would be $\frac{2}{5} \cdot \frac{1}{2}(+100) + \frac{2}{5} \cdot \frac{1}{2}(-50) + \frac{3}{5} \cdot \frac{1}{2}(0) + \frac{3}{5} \cdot \frac{1}{2}(+100) = +40$. And so on.

11. There is an interesting discussion of this problem in O. J. Bartos, *Simple Models of Group Behaviour*, pp. 187 ff.

give the same advice to Holmes, because from his point of view the two 'worst' payoffs are equally bad— +100 in each case. Possibly Holmes should just toss up after all!

We shall be talking about this problem again in the next chapter, and, I hope, gathering some of the threads together. In the meantime, let me mention yet another possibility—that the two men should treat the relevant probabilities as if they were certainties. Holmes, in other words, since the odds are in favour of Canterbury, should definitely get off there, and Moriarty should definitely get off at Dover. Interestingly enough, that is exactly what the two men in fact did in the story!

Suggestions for further reading

On the Theory of Games in General:
  Simple Models of Group Behavior, by O. J. BARTOS (Columbia University Press, 1967), parts 3 and 4
  The Compleat Strategyst, by J. D. WILLIAMS (McGraw-Hill Book Co., 2nd Edn., 1966)
  The Science of Decision-making, by ARNOLD KAUFMANN (Weidenfeld and Nicolson, 1968), chapter 5

On the Finger Game:
  A Guide to Operational Research, by ERIC DUCKWORTH (Methuen & Co., 1965), pp. 83–6

On the Holmes–Moriarty Game:
  The Final Problem, by SIR ARTHUR CONAN DOYLE (in *The Memoirs of Sherlock Holmes*)
  Theory of Games and Economic Behavior, by J. VON NEUMANN and O. MORGENSTERN (Princeton University Press, 1947), section 18.4.4

Chapter 10

How to beat General von Kluge and the forces of nature

In which a battle in the Second World War, and the strange case of the Jamaican fishermen, lead us to make a further exploration of the theory of games.

In August, 1944, shortly after the invasion of Normandy, the Allied forces broke out of their beachhead through a narrow gap at Avranches. The military situation as it then existed is shown in Figure 10.1[1].

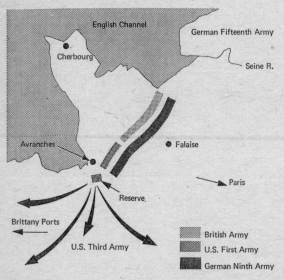

Figure 10·1

1. This diagram, and the one on p. 138 below, have been redrawn, by permission of the Operations Research Society of America, from two diagrams in the article upon which my account in the text is based: 'Military Decision and Game Theory', by O. G. Haywood, Jr. (*Journal of the Operations Research Society of America*, November, 1954).

It will be seen that the U.S. First Army and the British Army, having penetrated north-east of Avranches, were threatening the west flank of the German Ninth Army. The U.S. Third Army had moved south of Avranches and was beginning a wide sweep to the west, south, and east. A reserve of four U.S. Army divisions was standing just south of the gap, as yet uncommitted to action.

The commander of the U.S. forces was General Omar Bradley; and the commander of the German forces was General von Kluge. Each of these commanders was faced with the necessity of making a crucial tactical decision.

Von Kluge's choice lay between two alternatives: first, to *attack* towards the west in order to secure his west flank and cut off the U.S. Third Army; or, second, to *withdraw* to the east in order to take up a better defensive position near the River Seine.

General Bradley's problem related to the disposition of the uncommitted reserve standing south of the gap. His choice lay between three alternatives: first, *to order his reserve back to defend the gap*; second, *to send it eastward* to harass or possibly cut off the withdrawal of the German Ninth Army; or, third, *to leave it in position and uncommitted for one day*, moving it to the gap if necessary or eastward if the gap held without reinforcement.[2]

Thus in this 'game' there were six possible outcomes, which are set out in Figure 10.2. Let us discuss them here, not in the order in which they appear in the diagram, but in the order which they actually assumed in Bradley's scale of preferences, starting with the least desirable and gradually ascending to the most desirable:

1. Bradley sends the reserve eastward, and von Kluge attacks (the middle left-hand box in the diagram). There would then be a strong possibility that the Germans would break through, closing the gap and cutting off the U.S. Third Army. From Bradley's point of view this would obviously be a highly undesirable outcome.

2. According to Haywood, whom I am following closely here, 'Bradley reasoned before the battle started t hat, if the gap was attacked and held without reinforcement for the first day of attack, later reinforcement would be unnecessary.'

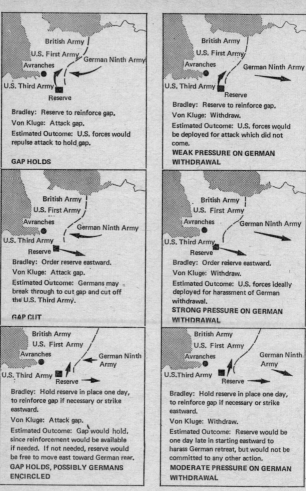

Figure 10·2

2. Bradley orders the reserve back to defend the gap, and von Kluge attacks (top left-hand box). The gap would hold, but there would be no pressure on any subsequent German withdrawal such as the reserve, if it had not been ordered back to defend the gap, might have exerted. This would be a more desirable outcome than the first one from Bradley's point of view, but it would be relatively undesirable as compared with the other possible outcomes discussed below.

3. Bradley orders the reserve back to defend the gap, and von Kluge withdraws (top right-hand box). The U.S. forces would then be deployed to meet a non-existent attack, and although *some* pressure could be exerted on the German withdrawal this would be relatively weak as compared with that which would be exerted in the case of the other possible outcomes discussed below.

4. Bradley leaves the reserve in position for one day, and von Kluge withdraws (bottom right-hand box). The pressure which could be exerted on the German withdrawal would be stronger than in the case of the third possible outcome just considered, but since the reserve would be one day late in starting eastward it would still be relatively weak as compared with that in the other possible outcomes discussed below.

5. Bradley sends the reserve eastward, and von Kluge withdraws (middle right-hand box). The U.S. forces would then be ideally deployed to exert pressure on the German withdrawal.

6. Bradley leaves the reserve in position for one day, and von Kluge attacks (bottom left-hand box). The gap would be bound to hold, since the reserve would be available if required to help defend it. And if it were not so required, it would be free to move east towards the German rear, with the distinct possibility of the encirclement and complete destruction of the German forces. From Bradley's point of view this would evidently be the most desirable of all the possible outcomes.

Let us now construct a payoff matrix for this game, using for the payoffs Bradley's *ordinal* figures ranging from one for the least preferable outcome to six for he most preferable.

The outcomes in the six boxes of the matrix correspond to those in the six compartments of Figure 10.2.

		General Von Kluge	
		attack	withdraw
General Bradley	reserve ordered back to gap	2	3
	reserve sent eastward	1	5
	reserve left in position for one day	6	4

Several instructive problems immediately arise. First, our games so far have all been, as it were, two-by-two, whereas this is three-by-two. Fortunately, however, it can be reduced immediately to a two-by-two game, since Bradley's first possible line of action—i.e., to order the reserve back to defend the gap—is clearly inferior, *whatever von Kluge does*, to his third possible line of action—i.e., to leave the reserve in position for one day. Obviously, therefore, Bradley would never pursue the first line of action, and the game reduces to one of the simple two-by-two type with which we are familiar:

		General Von Kluge	
		attack	withdraw
General Bradley	reserve sent eastward	1	5
	reserve left in position for one day	6	4

The second problem is rather less easy to deal with. The game has no saddle point,[3] so that mixed strategies are necessarily involved. But the optimum strategies for the participants in games of this sort, as we saw in the last chapter, depend on the *amounts* of the payoffs, whereas all that we are given here is the *order* of the payoffs. The strategies which emerge as the optimum ones in this game will differ according to the cardinal numbers to which these ordinal ones correspond. Thus suppose we take Bradley's ordinal numbers as true payoffs and not just rankings. Bradley's optimum strategy, worked out in the usual way—

	General Von Kluge		step one subtract the numbers in the second column from those in the first:	step two reverse the results, ignoring signs:
	attack	withdraw		
General Bradley — reserve sent eastward	1	5	$1 - 5 = -4$	2
reserve left in position for one day	6	4	$6 - 4 = 2$	4

would then be to play 'reserve sent eastward' and 'reserve left in position for one day' in the ratio 2:4, i.e., 1:2. Suppose, however, that Bradley *greatly* preferred the outcome in the bottom left-hand box to those in the other boxes, which in his mind were all bunched together preference-wise, and that the cardinal payoffs were in fact something like this:

	General Von Kluge	
	attack	withdraw
General Bradley — reserve sent eastward	5	7
reserve left in position for one day	20	6

3. See footnote 7 on p. 130 above.

In that case Bradley's optimum strategy, worked out in the same way, would be to play 'reserve sent eastward' and 'reserve left in position for one day' in the radically different ratio of 7:1. The moral of this is presumably that if we are going to be able to get anywhere near a determinate solution in problems of this kind we must not only know the order of the payoffs, but must also have at least some idea of their respective amounts.

The third problem is similar to the one we considered in the last chapter when we were discussing the Holmes–Moriarty conflict situation. Let us suppose that Bradley's ordinal numbers are in fact the true payoffs, so that the relevant strategies are:

For Bradley: Play 'reserve sent eastward' and 'reserve left in position for one day' in the ratio 1:2.

For von Kluge: Play 'attack' and 'withdraw' in the ratio 1:5.

According to the philosophy of the authors of the Theory of Games, both commanders should have played these strategies by the use of some kind of random device like counters in a hat. Bradley should have made the odds 2:1 in favour of 'reserve left in position for one day', and von Kluge should have made the odds 5:1 in favour of 'withdraw'.

Well, here we are again at the same old problem. This might well be the right thing to do if we were planning the overall strategy to be adopted in a large number of small and relatively unimportant battles. At the end of the last war, as Haywood points out in his article, the United States had some 600 batallion combat teams on the European continent, and it is at least arguable that if each commander had played the strategies prescribed by the Theory of Games by the use of a random device the overall results of this policy would have been good. But in the case of a single battle as important as that of Avranches, where you simply cannot afford the risk of loss, it would surely seem wrong to trust the fate of your forces—and maybe of the world—to counters in a hat.

Possibly this is a case where the appropriate prescription is to maximise your security level. Bradley should argue like this: 'If I left my reserve in position for one day, the worst that could happen from my point of view is that von Kluge would withdraw, in which case the outcome would be the one which comes third from the top of my scale of preferences. But if I sent my reserve eastward, the worst that could happen from my point of view is that von Kluge would attack, in which case the outcome would be the one which comes at the bottom of my scale of preferences. Therefore I should choose the better of these two "worsts" and leave my reserve in position for one day.' Von Kluge, on the basis of a similar 'play safe' argument, should obviously withdraw.

By another of those glorious strokes of luck which make the study of the Theory of Games so fascinating, *this is exactly what the two commanders in fact decided to do*. Bradley decided to leave his reserve in position for one day, and von Kluge to withdraw.

But this story has an ironical ending. After von Kluge had made his decision to withdraw, Hitler countermanded it and ordered him to attack. The outcome thus changed dramatically from that in the bottom right-hand box to that in the bottom left-hand box. Hitler, who was evidently unacquainted with the Theory of Games, handed Bradley the latter's best possible outcome on a plate. And this outcome really was realised. The gap held on the first day without reinforcement; the reserve was used to encircle the Germans; and after extricating the shattered remains of the German armies von Kluge committed suicide.

The upshot of all this, I think, is that the Theory of Games, at any rate in its original form, is of much more use to us in a many-game case than in a single-game case. So to help us restore our faith in the Theory, let us turn our attention now to a very remarkable real-world many-game case—that of the famous Jamaican fishermen, whose apparently intuitive knowledge of the Theory of Games was first brought to the attention of an astonished world by William Davenport in 1960.[4]

Davenport studied a fishing village of about 200 persons, located on the south shore of Jamaica. The male villagers, he tells us, are all fishermen, and they make their living exclusively by fishing in the local waters and selling their catches into the general marketing system of the island. Twenty-six fishing

4. *Jamaican Fishing: A Game Theory Analysis* (Yale University Publications in Anthropology, No. 59, 1960).

crews in sailing dugout canoes fish a large area adjacent to the shore by setting fish pots, which are drawn and reset, weather permitting, on three regular fishing days each week. The fishing crews are each composed of a captain, who owns the canoe, and two or three crewmen.

The fishing grounds, according to Davenport's account, are divided into inside and outside banks. The inside banks lie from 5 to 15 miles offshore, while the outside banks lie beyond. The distinction between inside and outside banks is not made solely on the basis of their distance from the shore, but also, more importantly, on the basis of the strength of the sea currents which flow across them. The outside banks are subject to very strong currents, which flow frequently but apparently quite unpredictably. The inside banks are almost fully protected from these currents.

The fishermen have three possible alternative lines of action. First, they can set all their pots *inside*. Second, they can set *some of their pots inside and some outside*. Third, they can set all their pots *outside*. The relative advantages and disadvantages of these three alternatives are governed by several different factors, of which the following are particularly important:

1. Fishing outside is more expensive in equipment than fishing inside. You need bigger and stronger canoes to go outside, and your pots are often swept away by the strong current when it is running. Thus your capital expenditure is higher.

2. To compensate for this, larger and better quality fish, and bigger catches, are obtainable on the outside banks—at any rate when the current is not running—than on the inside banks.

3. Supply-and-demand factors come into it as well. When the current is not running, and outside fishermen bring in large catches of quality fish, this drives the price of fish of lesser quality down, so that the inside fishermen suffer. Conversely, when the current *is* running, the absence of quality fish from outside enables the inside fishermen to force up the price of their poor quality fish, so that they do relatively well.

Clearly we can conceive of this as a two-person game in which the Village as a whole is playing against Nature. The Village has the three alternatives stated above, and Nature has two—*to send a current* or *not to send one*. Thus there are six possible outcomes, for which Davenport tried to work out the respective monetary payoffs. He did this by calculating what the average net income per canoe would be during a unit of time which he calls a 'fishing month' in each of the six possible eventualities. The result, putting it in the usual matrix form, was as follows:

		nature	
		current	no current
village	inside	£17.3	£11.5
	in and out	5.2	17.0
	outside	−4.4	20.6

The reader will notice that the figures in the first column go down, and that the figures in the second column go up—which is what we would expect from the geographical and economic conditions outlined above.

Given this payoff matrix, how should the Village play? There is a slightly sticky technical problem to deal with here before we can answer this.

The game is a three-by-two game, not a two-by-two game. And we cannot get over this in the simple way that we did in the Avranches case, because here there is no row *both* of the figures in which are smaller than those in some other row. So we have to use a gimmick. *It can be proved* that in all cases where you have two rows or columns and a number of columns or rows greater than two, the game always *contains* a particular two-by-two game the solution of which is in fact the solution of the larger game as a whole. The difficulty is to find it. Techniques for doing so are described in the books.[5] When

5. See, e.g., *The Compleat Strategyst*, a very readable book on the Theory of Games by J. D. Williams, pp. 65 ff.

we apply them to the present case, we find that the relevant two-by-two game is this:

	nature	
	current	no current
village — inside	£17.3	£11.5
in and out	5.2	17.0

As the reader will see, it is the same as the larger one except that the bottom row of the latter has been dropped.[6]

Under the circumstances, what would be the best strategy for the Village to adopt? According to the method of the Theory of Games, the Village's best strategy would be to play 'inside' and 'in and out' in the ratio 11·8:5·8. Or, to put

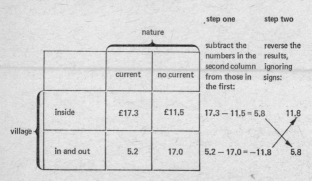

6. The reader can check this up for himself by working out the best strategy for Nature on the basis of this two-by-two game. Then, given this strategy for Nature, he can work out the returns which the Village would get from various different strategies involving combinations of 'inside', 'in and out', and 'outside'. He will find that it will get less from any strategy involving 'outside' than from any strategy *not* involving 'outside'. Thus the Theory of Games predicts that 'outside' is irrelevant. The Village ought not to adopt it at all, so we can simply strike it out.

the same thing in another way, the 26 canoes ought to be deployed in such a way that $\frac{11\cdot8}{11\cdot8 + 5\cdot8} \times 26$ of them (i.e., 17·45) are engaged in 'inside' fishing, and $\frac{5\cdot8}{11\cdot8 + 5\cdot8} \times 26$ of them (i.e., 8·55) are engaged in 'in and out' fishing. None of the canoes, as we have already seen, ought to engage in 'outside' fishing.

Having worked out what *ought* to happen, Davenport went down to have a look at what *did in fact* happen. *He found that during the periods of his observation 18 canoes were fishing 'inside', 8 were fishing 'in and out', and none were fishing 'outside'—i.e., the facts were in almost exact conformity with the prescriptions of the Theory of Games!*

Davenport now proceeded to work out from the payoff matrix the *best strategy of Nature*:

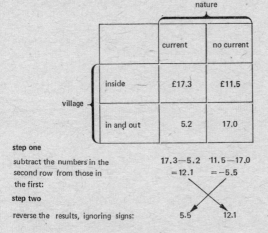

	nature	
	current	no current
inside	£17.3	£11.5
in and out	5.2	17.0

village

step one

subtract the numbers in the second row from those in the first:

17.3—5.2 = 12.1   11.5—17.0 = −5.5

step two

reverse the results, ignoring signs: 5.5   12.1

Nature, it turned out, ought to send a current about $\frac{5\cdot5 \times 100}{5\cdot5 + 12\cdot1}\%$ (i.e., about 31%) of the time. And once again Davenport checked up on what did in fact happen. 'Averaged estimates by fishermen for the years from June 1953 to June 1955,' he writes, 'yielded an "observed" proportion of 25% for the current.' Once again—although this time perhaps not *quite* as convincingly—the Theory of Games was confirmed.

Or was it? Let us just think for a moment about the possible implications of this last result. Nature, it appears, adopts something pretty close to that strategy which would minimise the Village's gains, in the face of the Village's best possible counter-strategy. In other words, Nature acts more or less as a conscious human player, anxious to do his opponent down, would act!

Unless one is a devil-worshipper or a believer in the male-volence of the gods, however, one simply cannot accept this implication. The proportion in which Nature sends and does not send sea currents in this area of the world can hardly be dictated by a desire to do down the inhabitants of a tiny fishing village on the south shore of Jamaica! It is pretty obvious that if there is some rough correspondence between the actual and the 'predicted' proportion this can be nothing more than a mere coincidence.

But it does raise a rather more important consideration. The prescribed strategy for the Village—to play 'inside', 'in and out', and 'outside' in the ratio 11·8:5·8:0—is only its optimum strategy if we assume that Nature is a conscious opponent who will always discover the Village's strategy and adopt the best possible counter-strategy. If in fact Nature is quite indifferent, sending a current 25% of the time for reasons of its own which have nothing to do with the fishermen, then it is quite open to the fishermen to move their own strategy away from the Theory of Games optimum *and adapt it to that of Nature* without any fear of the latter retaliating. And it is easy to show that in the present case they would in fact gain by doing this.

If the Village plays 'inside', 'in and out', and 'outside' in the ratio 11·8 : 5·8:0, and Nature plays 'current' and 'no current' in the ratio 1:3, the Village's expected gains can be easily calculated. If we assume, for the sake of simplifying the sums, that we are dealing with a total of 176 games, then the situation will be as follows:

	Nature's Play	Result
In $\frac{11 \cdot 8}{17 \cdot 6}$ of them ($= 118$) the Village plays 'inside'		
In $\frac{1}{4}$ of these ($= 29\frac{1}{2}$) Nature plays	'current'	$+510 \cdot 35$
In $\frac{3}{4}$ of these ($= 88\frac{1}{2}$) Nature plays	'no current'	$+1017 \cdot 75$
In $\frac{5 \cdot 8}{17 \cdot 6}$ of them ($= 58$) the Village plays 'in and out'		
In $\frac{1}{4}$ of these ($= 14\frac{1}{2}$) Nature plays	'current'	$+75 \cdot 40$
In $\frac{3}{4}$ of these ($= 43\frac{1}{2}$) Nature plays	'no current'	$+739 \cdot 50$
	Total gains of Village $=$	$+2343 \cdot 00$

This works out at an average expected gain of £13·29 per game.

But *given Nature's fixed 'strategy' of 1:3*, the Village could increase its average expected gains above £13·29 per game by moving from 11·8:5·8:0 to some other strategy. Suppose, for example, that it moved to 0:1:0—i.e., that it played 'in and out' every time. Out of every four games it would then gain £5·20 in one and £17·00 in the other three, so that its average gain would be $\frac{1}{4}$ (5·2) $+ \frac{3}{4}$ (17·0), i.e., £14·05, per game.

Or, still better, suppose that it moved to 0:0:1—i.e., that it played 'outside' every time. This is something that we have up to now assumed it would never do, so the reader will have to turn right back to p. 145 to find out the relevant payoffs. Out of every four games the Village would then lose £4·40 in one and gain £20·60 in the other three, so that its average gain would be $\frac{1}{4}$ (−4·4) $+ \frac{3}{4}$ (20·6), i.e. £14·35, per game.

So if in fact Nature is indifferent, and if in fact it plays 'current' and 'no current' in a 1:3 ratio, the Village is not at the moment acting rationally after all. It really ought to be doing all the time the one thing which it never does any of the time!

It is conceivable, of course, that the Village's strategy was worked out over a long period of years during which it was assumed that Nature *was* malevolent—in which case the strategy adopted was the 'right' one. By the time the Village eventually discovered that Nature was *not* malevolent but had a fixed strategy, it may be that the old practices had crystallised into a more or less inflexible tradition or custom which could not easily be changed. And anyway there would not have been much incentive to change: the difference between an average gain of £13·29 per game and one of £14·35 is hardly a very significant one—especially when we bear in mind the very big risks involved in fishing outside.[7]

And that, I think, is as far as we can take the Strange Case of the Jamaican Fishermen. Does it reveal an intuitive understanding of the Theory of Games on the part of these unsophisticated villagers, or is the whole thing just a gigantic coincidence? Clearly much more experimentation in this field will be necessary before we can come to any firm conclusions. But I hope that I have proved at any rate that a theory which can lead one to ask such interesting and important questions about real-world social conflict situations is well worth serious study by social scientists.

7. It should also be mentioned that the values Davenport puts on the payoffs, as he himself would be the first to admit, are by no means as accurate as the two places of decimals might suggest.

Suggestions for further reading

On the Case of the Battle of Avranches:
  'Military Decision and Game Theory', by O. G. HAYWOOD, JR. (*Journal of the Operations Research Society of America*, November 1954)
  Simple Models of Group Behavior, by O. J. BARTOS (Columbia University Press, 1967), chapter 11

On the Case of the Jamaican Fishermen:
  'Jamaican Fishing: A Game Theory Analysis', by W. DAVENPORT (*Yale University Publications in Anthropology*, No. 59, 1960)
  Game Theory in the Behavioral Sciences, ed. I. R. BUCHLER and H. G. NUTINI (University of Pittsburgh Press, 1969), introduction, and chapter 6

Chapter 11
The prisoner's dilemma

In which we study two more games—'Prisoner's Dilemma' and 'Chicken'—which are of particular interest in the field of social psychology.

There were once two prisoners who had been arrested and charged jointly with the same crime. They were held in separate cells, so that they were quite unable to communicate with one another. The prosecutor, realising that the case against them was weak, conceived a cunning scheme to get them to confess.

'Your companion in crime has not yet confessed,' he said to the first prisoner, 'so I shall be generous. If you confess and he does not, you will be set free and get a substantial money reward into the bargain.'

'And what would happen to the other man if I did?' asked the prisoner.

'He would get the book thrown at him. Five years at least, I would think,' replied the prosecutor.

'And what would happen if he confessed too?' asked the prisoner.

'In that case you would both get light sentences,' said the prosecutor.

'And suppose neither of us confessed?'

'I will be quite frank with you—in that case you would both have to be set free. Incidentally, I should probably tell you that I'm going to put exactly the same proposition before your companion.'

The first prisoner said he would think it over. The prosecutor then went to the second prisoner's cell, and had exactly the same conversation with him. He then went back to his quarters, and, chuckling fiendishly, sat down in front of his fire to await developments.

Let us set out the four possible outcomes in the form of a payoff matrix (see overleaf). The lower left entry in each box is the payoff to the first prisoner, and the upper right entry is the payoff to the second.

second prisoner

The actual figures I have put on the payoffs are of course purely notional, but their relative order of magnitude follows from the story. The payoff promised to the man who confesses when his companion does not ($+2$), which represents freedom plus a money reward, must obviously be higher than the payoff to each man when neither confesses ($+1$), which represents freedom alone. The latter payoff in its turn must be higher than the payoff to each man when they both confess (-1), which represents a light sentence. And finally this 'light sentence' payoff must be higher than the 'heavy sentence' payoff (-2) accruing to the man who does not confess when his companion does.

This is the Prisoner's Dilemma game—the most famous of all the so-called 'nonzero-sum' games. They are given this label to distinguish them from the games we considered in chapters 9 and 10, where the gains and lossess associated with each outcome always added up to zero. Nonzero-sum games, as we shall see almost immediately, raise all sorts of new and highly instructive problems.

What is the solution of the Prisoner's Dilemma game? If each prisoner decides to 'play safe', it is fairly clear that both will confess, so that they end up in the bottom right-hand box with each of them getting a light sentence. The first prisoner will argue like this: 'If my companion does not confess, I would do better by confessing ($+2$) than by not confessing ($+1$). And if my companion does confess, I would also do better by confessing (-1) than by not confessing (-2). Therefore I ought to confess.' And since the other prisoner will argue in exactly the same way, we finish up with both of them confessing.

Or do we? It is true that this is in a sense a 'rational' outcome, since confessing gives the higher payoff whatever the other party does; and it is true that it is also in a sense an 'equilibrium' outcome, since if either of the men confesses the other would do worse by not confessing than by confessing. But there is a novel feature about the present game which was not to be found in any of the other games we considered earlier. In this game, *both men could improve their position if they moved from the bottom right-hand box to the top left-hand box*. It may be 'rational' or 'prudent' for both of them to decide to confess, but they would do a lot better for themselves if they both decided not to confess. The very concept of 'rationality' upon which we have so far relied seems to be slipping through our fingers.

All right, neither confesses—is that the solution, then? It would not be an *equilibrium* solution, but it might well be what would in fact happen *if the two men could trust one another*. But the cunning prosecutor, having made it impossible for them to communicate with one another, has put a high premium on mutual distrust by promising $+2$ to the man who confesses when his companion does not, and -2 to the man who does not confess when his companion does. Each man is tempted by greed to double-cross his companion, and each man fears being double-crossed by him. The safest thing, obviously, is to confess—which is of course what the prosecutor counted upon.

A frivolous example, with no possible counterpart in real life? Let us go back to the matrix on page 152. For 'First Prisoner' we substitute 'First Country'; for 'Second Prisoner' we substitute 'Second Country'; and for 'Confess' in all four places we substitute 'Arm'. Does the matrix not look a little more realistic now? And rather terrifying?

Both countries could clearly gain by not arming, but the rewards for double-crossing and the penalties for being double-crossed are so great that they may well decide to 'play safe', like the prisoners, and finish up in the bottom right-hand box, spending large sums on armaments. Unless, of course, they can somehow learn to trust one another!

But the dangers involved in a situation of this kind may be even greater than those implicit in the particular matrix we have just considered. The final outcome if both countries arm may be a mutually destructive war between them, so that the negative payoffs in the bottom right-hand box fall from -1 to, say, -5. The penalty for arming when the other country arms (-5) is now heavier than the penalty for not arming when the other country arms (-2). When this is the case, the game changes in a rather subtle way, and its analysis becomes a little more complex. In recent game theory literature this kind of situation, so obviously replete with the sinister possibilities of double-crossing, brinkmanship, and appeasement, is simulated by the so-called Game of Chicken.

The typical payoff matrix in the Game of Chicken is similar to that in Prisoner's Dilemma except for that reversal in the order of magnitude of the negative payoffs which is referred to in the last paragraph. For example:

		second driver	
		to swerve	to continue on course
first driver	to swerve	+1 / +1	+2 / −2
	to continue on course	−2 / +2	−5 / −5

The context here is the familiar American 'game' in which two motor cars are driven towards one another on a collision course. If the first driver swerves in order to avoid a crash, while the second driver continues on course, then the second driver rises appreciably, and the first falls appreciably, in the esteem of his young contemporaries. If it is the second driver who swerves, then these gains and losses are reversed. If both drivers swerve, it is a draw, and insofar as they can be said to gain at all they both gain equally. If both continue on course they naturally crash, and both suffer a serious loss.

Looking at the Chicken matrix and comparing it with the original one in Prisoner's Dilemma, we may at first sight see a glimmer of hope. At any rate, we may say, the second of the two alternatives is no longer the 'prudent' choice, so that the parties are not led quite as inexorably as they seemed to be in Prisoner's Dilemma to the bottom right-hand box. The reversal of the relative order of magnitude of the negative payoffs makes all the difference here. Each player certainly prefers continuing on course to swerving if the other player swerves, but he prefers swerving to continuing on course if the other player continues on course. Indeed, there is an important sense in which swerving, rather than continuing on course, is the 'prudent' choice, since if you swerve your payoff cannot be less than -2, whereas if you continue on course it may be as low as -5. And if both parties make this 'prudent' choice they will find themselves in the top left-hand box, where the aggregate payoffs are higher than those associated with any of the other three possible outcomes.

But this situation is not an equilibrium one, and a rather subtle difficulty arises. The *prudent* choice—i.e., swerving—is not necessarily the *rational* choice. Indeed, a moment's thought will show that it is in fact only the rational choice if the other player is *im*prudent—i.e., continues on course. If A thinks that B is going to continue on course, then it will certainly be rational for A to swerve, since he will thereby lose -2 instead of -5. But if A thinks that B is going to swerve, then it is rational for A not to swerve, but to continue on course, since he will thereby gain $+2$ rather than $+1$. If, however, A assumes that B has come to the latter conclusion as well, then it will no longer be rational for him to continue on course, since the outcome would be a collision. We are clearly in the presence of a dilemma just as perplexing as that which faced our two prisoners.

One way of summing all this up is to say that in Prisoner's Dilemma the prudent choice leads to an outcome which represents an equilibrium, but does not maximise the payoffs. In Chicken, on the other hand, the prudent choice leads to an outcome which maximises the payoffs, but does not represent an equilibrium.[1] In nonzero-sum games of this kind prudence, rationality, and equilibrium may diverge, and it seems hopeless to try to find anything which could really pass as a 'solution'.

Why, then, are social scientists—and particularly social psychologists—so interested in games like Chicken and Prisoner's Dilemma? Because situations of the kind typified in these games, where the interests of the parties are partly opposed and partly in harmony, are much more common in the real world than the out-and-out conflict situations typified in zero-sum games. Even if we cannot find a meaningful 'solution' of these games, the social psychologists argue, we may be able to learn some very important lessons by studying the behaviour of people playing the games under test conditions in a laboratory. For the attitudes these people display when playing the games—attitudes of prudence and imprudence, dominance and submission, trust and lack of trust, and so on—may possibly be similar to the attitudes which people display in the real-world situations of conflict-plus-cooperation which these games in effect simulate.

The experiments which have been carried out in this field are quite fascinating. Rapoport and Chammah, for example, got a large number of pairs of University of Michigan students to play Prisoner's Dilemma about 300 times in succession, carefully recording each move. The students were shown a payoff matrix, and asked to start playing. They were not told the story of the prisoners; the two alternatives were labelled simply 'Left' and 'Right'. Each player selected one of the two alternatives without knowing the other player's choice; the outcome was announced and the moves recorded; and the game was repeated. The gains or losses accumulated by the players at the end of the experiment were converted into

1. This does not mean that there are no equilibrium outcomes in Chicken. The outcomes in the top right-hand and bottom left-hand boxes both represent situations from which one player cannot depart without impairing his payoff. And there is also a *mixed* strategy (3:1 in the case of the matrix in the text) from which, if both are playing it, neither can improve his position by departing. But none of these three outcomes are very satisfactory. The first and second may be equilibria, but they are hardly very *stable* equilibria, since one player is clearly dominating the other. And the expected gains per game in the third, although they are the same for both players ($\frac{1}{4}$ each in the assumed case), are conspicuously less than those obtainable from the 'prudent' outcome in the top left-hand box.

money at a prescribed rate per point, and added to or subtracted from the hourly pay they received for taking part. A few years later, Rapoport and Chammah conducted a similar experiment at the same University, this time with a Chicken matrix instead of a Prisoner's Dilemma one.

The basic idea lying behind these experiments is that the outcomes in the different boxes have different psychological or behavioural meanings. In Prisoner's Dilemma, for example, the outcome in the top left-hand box (neither prisoner confessing) suggests that the players are cooperating with one another. The outcome in the bottom right-hand box (both confessing) occurs if they are both 'playing safe'. The other two outcomes suggest that one player is trying to cooperate but the other is exploiting this. In Chicken, by way of contrast, it is the outcome in the top left-hand box (both swerving) which suggests that the players are 'playing safe'. The outcome in the bottom right-hand box (both continuing on course) suggests either that each player is trying to intimidate the other, or that one is refusing to give in to intimidation. The other two outcomes suggest dominance or intimidation of one player by the other.[2]

The experimenters are interested in such things as the frequency with which these different outcomes occur in the course of the game; the frequency with which a player changes his strategy, given any particular outcome; and the lengths of continuous runs of the different outcomes ('lock-ins', as they are called). And they are interested in particular in the causes of *changes* in these things. How does the frequency of the different outcomes change, for instance, as the number of plays of the game increases? And how far do alterations in the amounts of the payoffs, or in the way in which the payoffs are notified to the players, or in the sex of the players, cause changes in the frequency of the different outcomes?

What the experimenters are mainly trying to uncover, of course, are the factors that encourage cooperation, prudence, and trust and discourage intimidation and dominance—i.e., the factors that tend in the game to attract the players from the bottom right-hand box to the top left-hand one. The assumption is that if these factors do this in the game, they

2. See A. Rapoport, 'Games as Tools of Psychological Research', in *Game Theory in the Behavioral Sciences* (ed. I. R. Buchler and H. G. Nutini), p. 140.

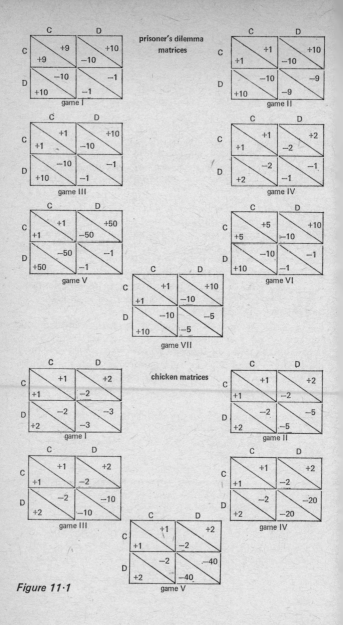

Figure 11·1

may also do it in conflict-plus-cooperation situations in the real world.

Rapoport and Chammah used seven different payoff matrices in their Prisoner's Dilemma experiment, and five in their Chicken experiment. These matrices are reproduced in Figure 11.1, where *C* stands for the *C*ooperative or *C*hicken alternative (not confessing in Prisoner's Dilemma; swerving in Chicken), and *D* stands for the *D*efecting or *D*aring alternative (confessing in Prisoner's Dilemma; continuing on course in Chicken). As will be seen, the payoffs in the case of Prisoner's Dilemma vary considerably from one matrix to another. In the case of Chicken the variations affect only the payoffs in the bottom right-hand box.

These variations in the payoffs had an appreciable effect on the choices made by the players. In the Prisoner's Dilemma experiment, for example, the frequencies of *C* choices (as a percentage of total choices) for the seven different games were as follows:[3]

Game	% of C Choices
I	73·4
II	77·4
III	45·8
IV	66·2
V	26·8
VI	63·5
VII	59·4

This is roughly what one would expect. The greatest percentage of *C* choices is found in Game II, where the penalty if both parties play *D* is very high. The smallest percentage is found in Game V, where the temptation to double-cross is very high. Looking at the picture as a whole, it appears that cooperation is increased by an increase in either of the payoffs associated with the *C* choice, and decreased by an increase in either of the payoffs associated with the *D* choice (the other payoffs being held constant).

3. These are the figures for what Rapoport and Chammah call the 'Pure Matrix Condition', in which a given pair of subjects plays the same game (not mixed with other games) throughout the whole run of 300 plays, and the subjects see the game matrix displayed.

In the Chicken experiment the position was broadly the same, but with one intriguing difference. The frequencies of *C* choices (as a percentage of total choices) for the five different games were as follows:

Game	% of C Choices
I	64
II	73
III	63
IV	77
V	81

Here, as one would expect, there is a general tendency for the frequency of *C* choices to increase as the penalty if both parties play *D* increases. But there is a reversal in this trend from game II to game III which cries out for an explanation. Rapoport and Chammah suggest that as the penalty increases there may be two pressures operating on the subjects: 'One is an increasing pressure to play *C*, since *D* entails a risk of a larger loss if *DD* should obtain. However, there may also be an increased pressure to play *D*, perhaps based on the belief that as the punishment for double defection becomes more severe, each player expects that the other will be reluctant to take the punishment associated with retaliation. On the other hand, when the punishment becomes excessive, the temptation to [play *D*] may be attenuated by the prospect of the great risk.'[4]

Could this possibly help to explain the intensification and subsequent relaxation of the so-called 'Cold War' since 1945, during the period when weapons of mass destruction have become progressively more fiendish? Rapoport and Chammah are wise enough not to suggest this: to argue directly from a simple game played for pennies in a laboratory to the macro-cosmic game of world politics would be merely silly. But the analogy is sufficiently striking, I think, to suggest that experiments of this kind may eventually be able to throw light on some of the really vital political problems of our time.

4. A. Rapoport and A. M. Chammah, 'The Game of Chicken', in *Game Theory in the Behavioral Sciences* (ed. I. R. Buchler and H. G. Nutini), p. 157.

Another interesting fact which emerges from the experiments is that it takes time to develop mutual trust, and that before the players learn to trust one another there may be a period when they learn to *dis*trust one another. In the Prisoner's Dilemma experiment, for example, the investigators combined the data obtained from all the games and measured the average frequency of the four different outcomes (*CC*, *CD*, *DC*, and *DD*) in successive runs of 15 plays—i.e., 1–15, 16–30, 31–45, etc. The results, so far as they relate to the *CC* and *DD* outcomes, are shown in Figure 11.2.[5]

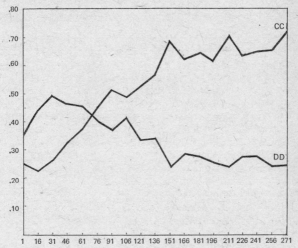

Figure 11·2

The early tendency, it will be seen, was for the frequency of *DD* outcomes to increase and that of *CC* outcomes to decrease. The cunning prosecutor would have rubbed his hands with glee: the players, as soon as they began to appreciate the hard realities of the situation, were led more and more frequently towards the 'rational' but punishing outcome in the bottom right-hand box. After about forty plays, however, they apparently began to realise that mutual trust, however 'irrational' it might be, would in fact pay off, and the two curves began

5. These results relate once again to the 'Pure Matrix Condition' (see the footnote on p. 159 above).

that startling change of direction which, as can be seen from the graph, continued more or less until the end of the game. We human prisoners, it would seem, are not quite such incurably suspicious creatures as the prosecutor thought: given time, we *can* learn to trust one another.

The results just described were those of games in which the payoff matrix was visibly displayed throughout. In another series of games, in which the payoff matrix was not actually displayed (although the payoffs were announced following each play, so that the players must very soon have known what they were), the results turned out to be startlingly different (see Figure 11.3).

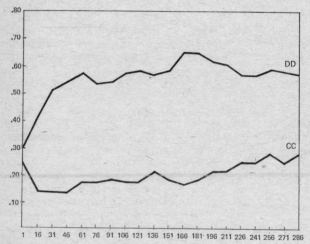

Figure 11·3

Here, as the reader will see, the initial rise in the frequency of *DD* outcomes is not reversed, but merely levels off, and the degree of cooperation shows very little tendency to increase. Comparing this case with the previous one, the moral would seem to be that when all the possibilities implicit in a conflict-plus-cooperation situation are kept constantly before our eyes, they serve to impress us with the benefits obtainable through cooperation rather than with those obtainable through double-crossing.

Equally spectacular were the differences in the frequencies of the *CC* and *DD* outcomes when men played men and when women played women. In the Chicken experiment, the results were as follows:

Game	Male Pairs		Female Pairs	
	CC	DD	CC	DD
I	48%	20%	46%	19%
II	60	14	54	17
III	48	23	36	27
IV	61	7	37	25
V	68	7	57	5

Women, it would appear, are appreciably less cooperative and trustful of one another in conflict-plus-cooperation situations than men! And in the Prisoner's Dilemma experiment it was much the same story. When men played men, the average frequency of *C* choices was 59%; when women played women it was only 34%.

But what happens when women play against men? In Prisoner's Dilemma, Rapoport and Chammah report, 'we find that women are "pulled up" when playing against men, that is, they play more cooperatively against men than against women. Men, on the contrary, are "pulled down" when playing against women as compared with their performance against players of their own sex. However, the men are not pulled down as much as the women are pulled up. In general, the performance of mixed groups is squarely between the performance of the men and of the women, rather nearer that of men.'[6] Take out of that what you will!

Enough has been said, I hope, to suggest that research into these nonzero-sum games may have quite a future. Obviously it has its limitations: the way in which statesmen behave at times of international crisis may be very different from the way they would behave if they were playing Chicken in a laboratory at the University of Michigan. Perhaps this research will always be more productive of new questions than of new answers. But in the world as it is today any investigation of the conditions under which mutual trust between

6. A. Rapoport and A. M. Chammah, *Prisoner's Dilemma*, p. 191.

human beings may be strengthened and maintained must surely be welcome.

Suggestions for further reading

On Prisoner's Dilemma:

Prisoner's Dilemma, by A. RAPOPORT and A. M. CHAMMAH (University of Michigan Press, 1965)

'Games as Tools of Psychological Research', by A. RAPOPORT (in *Game Theory in the Behavioral Sciences*, ed. I. R. BUCHLER and H. G. NUTINI, University of Pittsburgh Press, 1969)

Simple Models of Group Behavior, by O. J. BARTOS (Columbia University Press, 1967), chapter 12

On Chicken:

'The Game of Chicken', by A. RAPOPORT and A. M. CHAMMAH (in *Game Theory in the Behavioral Sciences*, ed. I. R. BUCHLER and H. G. NUTINI)

On Game Theory and the Study of Social Behaviour in General:

Game Theory and Related Approaches to Social Behavior, ed. MARTIN SHUBIK (John Wiley & Sons, 1964)

Chapter 12
Counting the cost

In which we learn something about the theory, techniques, and applications of cost-benefit analysis.

Cost-benefit analysis is a phenomenon, like Mr. Enoch Powell, which possesses a peculiar capacity to provoke wide differences of opinion about its utility. To some people, it appears as a revolutionary new technique which is removing subjectivism and arbitrariness from government decision-making and replacing them by objective judgement and scientific rationality. To other people, the whole thing is an ill-advised attempt to measure the immeasurable: the most it can do, they claim, is to provide a certain amount of partisan support in the service of particular interests. This is one of those issues upon which we all have to make up our minds, because whether we like it or not cost-benefit analysis is obviously here to stay, and is rapidly extending its field of operation. Beginning in water resource development, it is now being widely employed in military planning, electricity supply, transport, land usage, education, and health. For better or for worse, it is affecting the daily lives of all of us, and it behoves us to know something about it.

There is as yet no settled definition of cost-benefit analysis, and we must therefore build up our picture of it by looking at what people who call themselves cost-benefit analysts actually do. Basically, we find, what they are all seeking, in one context or another, is a solution to the problem of making a rational choice between alternative courses of action. The particular techniques which they employ to this end usually involve (*a*) the assessment of the respective *costs and benefits* of the alternatives, and (*b*) the formulation and application of *criteria of choice* which are designed to discriminate between the alternatives on the basis of the *net* benefits (in some sense) associated with them.

But this description as it stands is too general by far. When we think about it, we see that it could probably be regarded as including the greater part of what commonly goes under the name of Operations Research—from which, at any rate up to a point, cost-benefit analysis has in fact succeeded in separating itself out. It has done this by concentrating its attention on a particular range of problems possessing three distinguishing characteristics.

First, the 'alternative courses of action' in which it is primarily interested are alternative *investment projects*—whence the other name that is sometimes given to it, 'project appraisal'. Second, it is particularly concerned with the complications which ensue when *time* comes into the picture in a big way—which it usually does when investment projects are being appraised, since such projects normally involve a *stream* of costs and benefits over a period which may extend into the quite distant future. And third, it is particularly interested in cases where there are important divergencies between the *private* and the *social* costs and benefits associated with a project.

These three characteristics of the problems which are the special concern of cost-benefit analysis are partly the cause and partly the effect of its very close association with decision-making in the *public sector*. The immense growth of the public sector in many countries during the last thirty or forty years has brought about a large increase in the proportion of total annual investment for which the public authorities are responsible—and accountable. Nationalised industries are generally great users of capital, and the investment projects which they undertake are often so large and important that their effects extend in space far beyond the immediate range of operations, and in time far into the future. It is true, of course, that large investment projects in the private sector may also have important repercussions over space and time; and the growth in private industry of *capital budgeting* techniques, which have much in common with the techniques of cost-benefit analysis, has been quite considerable in recent years. But in cost-benefit analysis we are concerned with maximising social well-being rather than private profit, so that the repercussions which capital budgeting neglects are precisely those upon which cost-benefit analysis concentrates. In this chapter, therefore, we shall deal with cost-benefit analysis more or less exclusively in the context of the appraisal of *public* investment projects.

In discussing cost-benefit analysis, it is useful to break it down into two parts:

Part A: The aim here is to calculate, and present in as useful a manner as possible, all the costs (or disadvantages) and all the benefits (or advantages) involved in the different investment projects being considered. Since it is a public authority which is making the decision, it is presumably aiming at the well-being of society as a whole, which means that social as well as private costs and benefits have to be brought into account.

Part B: Having supplied ourselves with a balance-sheet of costs and benefits in respect of each of the projects, the task in Part B is to develop some kind of criterion on the basis of which a rational choice between them can be made. The general aim which such a criterion must fulfil is usually easy enough to formulate: it will normally be to *economise* in some sense—e.g., to use a given amount of capital as effectively as possible, or to produce a given stream of benefits with the least possible total expenditure of resources. But it is not nearly so easy to give specific content to this general aim and to apply it to particular cases, especially when time is an important factor.

So far as Part A is concerned, the main problems involved will be briefly reviewed under four headings.

(1) INTANGIBLES

These are particular benefits or costs whose magnitude cannot be expressed in terms of the main unit of measurement we are using (normally money). Suppose, for example, that the North of Scotland Hydro-electric Board wants to increase its output of electricity by some given amount, and its engineers tell it that this can be done *either* by a hydro-electric plant to be located in Glen Nevis, *or* by a rather more expensive hydro-electric plant to be located in some less picturesque spot—the Moor of Rannoch, say. Presumably if the Board's choice is to be rational it ought to include among the costs associated with the first project an item labelled something like 'Damage to people's aesthetic sensibilities caused by the decrease in the beauty of Glen Nevis'. But how could it possibly *quantify* this cost, in such a way as to make the total costs of the Glen Nevis project comparable with those of the Moor of Rannoch project?

When faced with this kind of problem, some people suggest that if we try hard enough we can in fact put a money value on everything. For example, it is argued, the saving of a human life may appear to be a highly intangible benefit, but in actual fact a money value *can* be put on it, on the basis of the awards which the courts give in the case of accidental death. If the saving of a human life is quantifiable in money terms, then, why not the beauty of Glen Nevis? Other people, however, argue that if a thing cannot be freely bought and sold the attribution of a money value to it must always be at least to some extent arbitrary, and may in many cases be very misleading indeed.

The truth no doubt lies somewhere between these two extremes. On the one hand, it is probably true that attempts to put a precise and really meaningful money value on the saving of a human life—or on the beauty of Glen Nevis—will never be very successful. On the other hand, considerable progress has been made in recent years in attributing sensible money values to certain things which many of us formerly regarded as intangibles—the saving of time caused by the building of a new road, for example, and the benefit derived from a university education; and it would be rash to prophesy that this progress had now reached its limit. And in any event it is a mistake to think that the non-quantifiability of at any rate *some* intangibles is necessarily fatal to cost-benefit exercises. If the analyst abstracts from these intangibles in his main balance-sheet of costs and benefits, but presents the decision-makers with a separate report on them, they can at least be seen in proper perspective, and it is amazing what a difference this can sometimes make.

(2) UNCERTAINTIES

Uncertainties are likely to be particularly important when we are comparing alternative investment projects with streams of costs and benefits which extend for a long period into the future. Suppose, for example, that we are comparing a projected hydro-electric station with a projected coal-fired station. The future benefits from the hydro-electric station will depend upon future rainfall, which is uncertain. The future costs of the coal-fired station will depend upon the future price of coal, which is also uncertain. But these two uncertainties are of different types. The first can be dealt with quite adequately on a probabilistic basis, by examining past trends of rainfall and extrapolating them into the future. We may not be able to say what the rainfall, and therefore the output of the station, will be in any particular year of its life, but we will certainly be able to predict pretty accurately what the *average* annual rainfall, and therefore the *average* annual output of the station, will be over its life as a whole. The second type of uncertainty, however, cannot be dealt with in this manner. All that the cost-benefit analyst can do is to put forward a number of different *hypotheses* about what the price of coal will be in the future, and make a different calculation of costs on the basis of each hypothesis. Sometimes it may be found that the result is the same, so far as the final decision is concerned, whichever of the hypotheses is adopted. If this turns out not to be the case, the decision-makers have to make the best bet which is possible under the circumstances, assisted by the techniques of *decision theory*.[1]

(3) MONEY COSTS AND BENEFITS AND REAL COSTS AND BENEFITS
The *costs* of a project are very often reckoned, at least in the first instance, in terms of the *money prices* paid for the resources used to construct and operate it. The *benefits* of a project are often reckoned, in the first instance, in terms of the *money prices* which consumers are prepared to pay for its product. And these *money* prices may not accurately reflect the *real* costs and benefits involved, which are what ought properly to be taken into account.

Take the case of an oil-fired power station, for example: the money cost to the electricity authorities of the oil which is used as fuel includes a substantial tax which is imposed by the Government in the interests of the coal industry. It may be argued, however, that this money cost over-estimates the *real* cost of the oil by the amount of the tax, which ought properly to be deducted when comparisons between this station and other alternative stations are being made.

Somewhat similar difficulties may have to be faced on the

1. *Decision theory* is not specifically dealt with in this book, although it makes considerable use of the *theory of games*, which has already been discussed above. A good introductory outline of some of the techniques involved will be found in *Economic Theory and Operations Analysis*, by W. J. Baumol, chapter 24.

benefits side of the balance-sheet. Suppose, for example, that we are comparing two projects, A and B, for which the costs are the same, but for which the benefits, *as measured by the prices which people are prepared to pay for the respective products*, are different. Should we choose the project with the greater surplus of benefits (as so measured) over costs? The answer may well be 'yes' if both groups of people have roughly the same income; but if they have very different incomes it may well be 'no'. Measurement of benefits in terms of market prices, in other words, may give misleading results unless we take account of the fact that the same amount of money may mean different amounts of *utility* to people with different incomes.

(4) INDIRECT BENEFITS AND COSTS

The point here is simply that in our calculations we must try to take account not only of the *direct* effects of the project but also of its *indirect*, or 'spillover' effects. For example, a river project which uses water upstream may reduce the production possibilities of power plants or irrigation facilities downstream. Or, to take the case of an indirect *benefit*, the building of an underground line may help to relieve traffic congestion in the streets above. These indirect costs or benefits should obviously be debited or credited to the project concerned. The difficulties involved here are twofold—how to value the indirect costs or benefits, and where to draw the line in including them.

Some of these difficulties will be referred to again later. Let us leave them aside for the time being—noting only that they have not prevented the successful application of cost-benefit analysis over a very wide field—and proceed immediately to Part B. We have worked out all the costs and benefits of a number of alternative investment projects, let us imagine, and now have to decide what the *criterion of choice* between them ought to be.

To select the appropriate criterion, we have first to decide whether the projects concerned are *mutually exclusive* or *independent*. The choice between some projects may be of the 'either–or' type. Our engineers, for example, may present us with two possible ways of using a single site—a large hydro-electric station or a small hydro-electric station at a single point on a river, for instance. These are obviously *mutually-exclusive* projects—we may select one or other of them, if we wish, but not both. Other projects presented to us, by way of contrast, may be quite separate from one another—two schools, for example, in two different parts of the country, under conditions where the demand for school education is expanding. These are obviously *independent* projects—it is open to us, if we wish, to select both. There may of course be cases which are intermediate between these two extremes, but for our purposes here we may ignore them.

The other thing we have to know is how much capital we shall be able to command in order to build the project or projects. Once again there are two extreme possibilities—either that we are faced with *capital rationing*, in the sense that we have a fixed and limited amount of capital at our disposal (the amount allocated to a Department by the Government, for example); or that there is *no capital rationing*, meaning by this (in most cases) that we have free access to the capital market and can borrow as much money as we want to at the current market rate of interest.

Thus there are four possible situations which may confront us:

1. The projects are independent, and there is no capital rationing.

2. The projects are independent, and capital is rationed.

3. The projects are mutually exclusive, and there is no capital rationing.

4. The projects are mutually exclusive, and capital is rationed.

It is important to distinguish between these four cases because, as we shall see, the criterion which we use may depend upon the particular case we are dealing with.

The criteria generally employed in cost-benefit analysis are constructed out of one or other of two important building-blocks: (*a*) the concept of the *present worth* of a project; and (*b*) the concept of the *internal rate of return* of a project. Both these basic concepts involve in one way or another the technique of finding the *present value* of sums of money falling due for payment or receipt in the future, and we shall therefore deal briefly with this technique before we discuss the building-blocks themselves.

Our main job in cost-benefit analysis is to compare alternative investment projects whose respective costs and benefits may be spread out in different ways over time. We must, therefore, find a technique for putting these temporal flows or streams of payments and receipts on to a common basis, so that they can be readily compared with one another. The only possible way of doing this is to reduce them to what is called in the arithmetic books their *present value*.

The present value of a given sum (£A) due to be received or paid a given number of years (n) from now, at a given *discount rate* ($r\%$), is defined as the sum (£P) which, if lent out now for n years at $r\%$ compound interest, would amount to £A at the end of the period. Thus suppose that a sum of £121 is due to be received or paid in two years' time, and that we decide to use a discount rate of 10%. The present value of this sum of £121, at this discount rate of 10%, will be £100, because £100 is the sum which, if lent out now for two years at 10% compound interest, would amount to £121 at the end of the period.[2]

To work out the present value of any given future sum is simplicity itself. We use the formula

$$P = \frac{A}{(1 + r)^n}$$

where P is the present value of the future sum, A is the future sum itself, r is the discount rate (here expressed decimally, and *not* as a percentage), and n is the number of years. Thus in the case we have just considered

$$P = \frac{A}{(1 + r)^n} = \frac{121}{(1 \cdot 1)^2} = 100$$

If we have a *stream* of benefits (or costs) falling due for receipt (or payment) over a period of years, we work out the present value of the stream by applying this formula to each of the individual items in it and adding the results. Thus suppose we have a project which will last for three years, and which will yield the following benefits:

2. At the end of the first year, the 10% interest earned on the initial sum of £100 would be added to this sum, making a total of £100 + 10% of £100 = £110. At the end of the second year, the 10% interest earned on this sum of £110 would be added on, making a total of £110 + 10% of £110 = £121.

	End of 1st Year		*End of 2nd Year*		*End of 3rd Year*
Benefits:	80	+	120	+	110

Let us assume that we adopt a rate of discount of 10%—i.e., 0·1 when expressed decimally.[3] The present value of the stream of benefits will then be

$$\text{P.V.} = \frac{80}{1\cdot1} + \frac{120}{(1\cdot1)^2} + \frac{110}{(1\cdot1)^3}$$

$$= 72\cdot7 + 99\cdot2 + 82\cdot6 = 254\cdot5$$

We may now turn our attention to the two building-blocks out of which the available criteria are constructed—each of which, as I have already said, involves in one way or another the calculation of the present value of future costs and benefits.

(1) PRESENT WORTH

The *present worth* of a project may be defined as the present value of the benefits which it will yield *minus* the present value of the costs which its construction and operation will involve.

Let us take a simple, if rather unrealistic, example. A project lasting two years will involve us, let us say, in an initial capital investment (I) for construction purposes of £100. Operating costs payable at the end of the first year (C_1) will be £110; and operating costs payable at the end of the second year (C_2) will be £121. The benefits accruing from the project at the end of the first year (B_1) will be £220; and the benefits accruing at the end of the second year (B_2) will be £242. This situation is summed up in the following table:

	Beginning of 1st Year	*End of 1st Year*	*End of 2nd Year*
Costs:	$I = £100$	$C_1 = £110$	$C_2 = £121$
Benefits:	—	$B_1 = £220$	$B_2 = £242$

3. The question of the rate of discount which we *ought* to adopt in such calculations in cost-benefit analysis is discussed below, pp. 182–4. Obviously this is very important, if only because the present value will depend materially on the particular rate we choose. The higher the rate the lower the present value, and vice versa.

What will the *present worth* of this project be, at a rate of discount of, say, 10%? The present worth is defined as the present value of the benefits minus the present value of the costs of construction and operation. Applying our present value formula, then, the present worth of the project, in symbolic terms, will be[4]

$$\frac{B_1}{1+r} + \frac{B_2}{(1+r)^2} - \left(I + \frac{C_1}{1+r} + \frac{C_2}{(1+r)^2}\right)$$

Substituting the values in our example, we get

$$\begin{aligned}
\text{Present Worth} &= \frac{220}{1\cdot1} + \frac{242}{(1\cdot1)^2} - \left(100 + \frac{100}{1\cdot1} + \frac{121}{(1\cdot1)^2}\right) \\
&= 200 + 200 - (100 + 100 + 100) \\
&= \pounds100
\end{aligned}$$

Generalising this for the case where the project lasts for n years, the present worth is given by the formula

$$\frac{B_1}{1+r} + \frac{B_2}{(1+r)^2} + \frac{B_3}{(1+r)^3} + \cdots \frac{B_n}{(1+r)^n}$$

$$- \left(I + \frac{C_1}{1+r} + \frac{C_2}{(1+r)^2} + \frac{C_3}{(1+r)^3} + \cdots \frac{C_n}{(1+r)^n}\right)$$

Or, regrouping the terms, it is given by the formula

$$\frac{B_1 - C_1}{1+r} + \frac{B_2 - C_2}{(1+r)^2} + \frac{B_3 - C_3}{(1+r)^3} + \cdots \frac{B_n - C_n}{(1+r)^n} - I$$

This way of putting it shows that the present worth of a project is really the amount by which the present value of the flow of *net returns* (i.e., benefits minus operating costs) exceeds the initial capital investment.

Given the values for I, for n, and for all the $(B - C)$'s, the present worth of a project will clearly depend on the value of r—i.e., on the particular rate of discount which we use in the

---

4. The assumption here is that the benefits fall due for receipt, and the operating costs fall due for payment, at the *end* of each year. The amount of the initial capital investment, on the other hand, is assumed to be paid out at the *beginning* of the first year, so that the present value of this amount is equal to the amount itself.

calculations. Suppose that we work out the present worth of
the two-year project we have just been considering at various
rates of discount ranging from 0% to 100%, and plot the
results on a graph in which the rate of discount is measured
along the horizontal axis and the present worth is measured
up the vertical axis. If we join up the points, we will get the
curve in Figure 12.1.

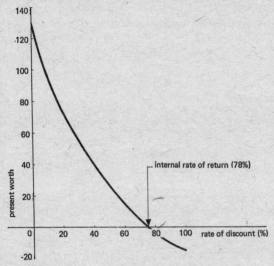

Figure 12·1

When the rate of discount is zero, the present value of the
flow of net returns will be equal to the sum of the net returns
themselves—i.e., it will be £110 + £121 = £231, which
exceeds the initial capital investment by £131. Our curve will
therefore begin at 131 on the vertical axis. As the rate of discount rises above zero, the present value of the flow of net
returns will decrease, so that the amount by which it exceeds
the initial capital investment (i.e., the amount of the present
worth of the project) will also decrease Eventually, as the rate
of discount continues to rise, there will come a point at which
the present value of the flow of net returns will be just equal
to the initial capital investment, so that the present worth of

the project is zero. At this point—which is reached in our example when the rate of discount is about 78%—the curve will cut the horizontal axis, thereafter falling below it.

(2) INTERNAL RATE OF RETURN

The internal rate of return of a project is usually defined as the rate of discount which would make the present value of the benefits of the project equal to the present value of its costs of construction and operation. In the general case of a project lasting n years, therefore, it is given by the value of i in the equation

$$\frac{B_1}{1+i} + \frac{B_2}{(1+i)^2} + \frac{B_3}{(1+i)^3} + \cdots \frac{B_n}{(1+i)^n}$$

$$= I + \frac{C_1}{1+i} + \frac{C_2}{(1+i)^2} + \frac{C_3}{(1+i)^3} + \cdots \frac{C_n}{(1+i)^n}$$

Or, regrouping the terms, it is given by the value of i in the equation

$$\frac{B_1 - C_1}{1+i} + \frac{B_2 - C_2}{(1+i)^2} + \frac{B_3 - C_3}{(1+i)^3} + \cdots \frac{B_n - C_n}{(1+i)^n} = I$$

In the case of our two-year project, for example, the internal rate of return will be given by the value of i in the equation

$$\frac{B_1 - C_1}{1+i} + \frac{B_2 - C_2}{(1+i)^2} = I$$

Substituting the actual values concerned, we get the equation

$$\frac{220 - 110}{1+i} + \frac{242 - 121}{(1+i)^2} = 100$$

and when we work out the value of i in this equation[5] we find that it comes out at approximately 0·78, or 78%.

The fact that the internal rate of return in this case is equal to the rate of discount which would bring the present worth of the project out at zero (see top of page) is not a coincidence. This will necessarily be true in all cases. For, as we already know, if we work out the present worth of a project using a

5. The equation is a *quadratic* one—i.e., one of the general type $ax^2 + bx + c$. A formula for solving equations of this type will be found in any elementary algebra book.

particular rate of discount r, and the result happens to come out at zero, the present value of the flow of net returns will be just equal to the initial capital investment—in other words, the following equality will necessarily obtain

$$\frac{B_1 - C_1}{1 + r} + \frac{B_2 - C_2}{(1 + r)^2} + \frac{B_3 - C_3}{(1 + r)^3} + \cdots \frac{B_n - C_n}{(1 + r)^n} = I$$

And, as we have just seen, the internal rate of return is given by the value of i in the equation

$$\frac{B_1 - C_1}{1 + i} + \frac{B_2 - C_2}{(1 + i)^2} + \frac{B_3 - C_3}{(1 + i)^3} + \cdots \frac{B_n - C_n}{(1 + i)^n} = I$$

If we now compare the equality with the equation, we see immediately that the internal rate of return, as defined above, must necessarily be equal to the rate of discount which would bring the present worth of the project out at zero. This is an important point, which will be referred to again later.

The internal rate of return (or the yield, or rate of return *simpliciter*, as it is sometimes called) is a measure of the *rate of return on capital* which the flow of net returns from the project represents. Take the case of our two-year project, in which $I = 100$, $B_1 - C_1 = £110$, and $B_2 - C_2 = £121$, and in which the internal rate of return works out at 78%. It is easy to show that the net returns of £110 and £121 represent a rate of return of 78% on the initial capital of £100. For suppose that a man lent out £100 for a year at 78% interest. At the end of the year £178 would be due to him. Suppose he took £110 (corresponding to the first year's net returns from the project) out of this sum, and lent out the remaining £68 for a further year at 78% interest. At the end of the second year the amount due to him would be almost exactly £121,[6] corresponding to the second year's net returns from the project. Thus the internal rate of return, worked out as we have indicated above, measures the rate of return on capital which the flow of net returns from the project represents.

We are now in a position to use these two building-blocks in

6. £68 + 78% of £68 = £121·04. The correspondence is not exact because the internal rate of return in this case is in fact a tiny fraction below 78%.

order to construct the appropriate criteria for use in the four cases which we distinguished above, viz.

1. Projects independent, no capital rationing.

2. Projects independent, capital rationed.

3. Projects mutually exclusive, no capital rationing.

4. Projects mutually exclusive, capital rationed.

We assume that in each case the general aim of the criterion we select should be to maximise the total surplus of benefit over cost achievable in the given circumstances, *subject to the constraint that the rate of return yielded by any project selected should never be less than some prescribed minimum.* This proviso is necessary because we assume, quite realistically, that the public authority concerned will lay down some minimum acceptable rate of return which new investment projects must yield before it will consider them as qualifying for selection.

1. PROJECTS INDEPENDENT, NO CAPITAL RATIONING

When the projects are independent, and the enterprise's access to capital is unlimited, there are two alternative modes of procedure which it may adopt. *First*, it may begin by working out the present worth of each project, using a rate of discount equal to the prescribed minimum rate of return. If the present worth when so calculated turns out to be positive (i.e., >0), this means that the rate of return yielded by the project must be greater than the rate of discount used in the calculation [7]— i.e., in the present case, greater than the prescribed minimum rate of return, so that the project qualifies for selection. And if it qualifies for selection—by however great or small a margin—it should (in this first case) in fact be selected, since if it is not carried out the *total* surplus of benefit over cost achievable in the given circumstances will not be maximised. The criterion of choice is therefore: 'Carry out all projects

7. A glance back at Figure 12·1 will show that this must be so. When the curve cuts the horizontal axis, so that present worth is zero, the project's rate of return is equal to the rate of discount used. To the left of this point, where present worth is >0, the project's rate of return must be greater than the rate of discount used.

which show a positive present worth at a discount rate equal to the prescribed minimum rate of return.'

Second, it may begin by working out the internal rate of return of each project. The criterion of choice will then be: 'Carry out all projects for which the internal rate of return is greater than the prescribed minimum rate of return.' This second procedure will give the same result as the first, since projects for which the internal rate of return is greater than the prescribed minimum rate of return will necessarily show a positive present worth at a discount rate equal to the prescribed minimum rate of return;[8] and their selection will therefore add to the *total* surplus of benefit over cost achievable in the given circumstances.

Which is the better of these two criteria—that based on present worth or that based on the internal rate of return? In the context of the first of our four cases, and in most normal circumstances, there is not really very much to choose between them. Under certain rather special circumstances, however, when we work out the value of i in the internal rate of return equation we may get two (or even more) different values instead of one unique value,[9] and even if this is not quite so serious a consideration as it is sometimes made out to be it helps to swing the balance towards the criterion based on present worth.

2. PROJECTS INDEPENDENT, CAPITAL RATIONED

When the projects are independent but capital is rationed, the projects must somehow be ranked, in order of merit. In the case we have just considered, no ranking in this sense was necessary: our two criteria were required merely to divide the projects into the sheep and the goats—into those which would add to the total surplus of benefit over cost (subject to the given constraint) and those which would not. If we have a limited budget at our disposal, however, and want to maximise the total surplus of benefit over cost achievable under the given circumstances, we ought obviously to carry out the most 'profitable' projects first—which implies putting the projects in some kind of order of merit.

8. Once again a glance at Figure 12.1 will show that this must be true. If the rate of discount selected is less than the internal rate of return, the present worth of the project will necessarily be positive.

9. See the Mathematical Appendix, section 12, pp. 227–9.

At first sight, it might seem that we ought to rank them in accordance with the *amount* of return (in some sense or other) which they will yield, and then simply go down the list until the budget is exhausted. Take, for example, the following case, where five projects have been ranked on the basis of the respective amounts of their present worths:

	Initial Capital	Present Worth
A	250	26
B	250	25
C	200	24
D	200	22
E	100	20

If we had a total of, say, 500 capital available, it might seem that the proper procedure would be to proceed down this list until the budget of 500 was exhausted, which would mean that we would adopt projects A and B. But we could obtain a greater total present worth (and thus a greater total surplus of benefit over cost) in this case by adopting C, D, and E instead of A and B. The correct choice will not be indicated unless we re-rank the projects according to some kind of *rate*-of-return measure.

There are a number of such measures which are available. One is, of course, the internal rate of return, which we might well use if we felt that there was no danger of dual values for i emerging from the equation. Another is *present worth per unit of capital investment*, which is simply the present worth (defined and calculated as described above) expressed as a ratio, or percentage, of the initial capital investment.[10] If we

10. Present worth per unit of capital investment will not normally work out the same as the internal rate of return. Figure 12.1 may help to clarify this. In the project to which the diagram refers, the initial capital is 100. When the rate of discount is zero, the present worth is 131, so that present worth per unit of capital investment will be 131/100, or 131%. When the rate of discount is 10%, present worth per unit of capital investment will be 100/100, or 100%. When the rate of discount is 40%, present worth per unit of capital investment will be 40·31/100, or 40·31%. Only for one rate of discount in this range (about 19%) will the present worth per unit of capital investment be equal to the internal rate of return.

used the latter measure to re-rank the five projects, the result
would be as follows:

	Initial Capital	*Present Worth*	*P. W. Per Unit of Initial Capital*
E	100	20	20%
C	200	24	12%
D	200	22	11%
A	250	26	10·4%
B	250	25	10%

Going down *this* list until our budget is exhausted does give
us the right answer.

Since we must be careful not to accept any projects which
would earn less than the prescribed minimum rate of return,
it is possible that we may have to stop at some point *before*
the budget is exhausted. If we rank the projects according to
the present worth per unit of initial capital investment, using
a rate of discount equal to the prescribed minimum rate of
return, this cut-off point will be reached when the present
worth has fallen to zero. If we rank them according to the
internal rate of return, the cut-off point will be reached when
this rate has fallen to equality with the prescribed minimum
rate.

3. PROJECTS MUTUALLY EXCLUSIVE, NO CAPITAL RATIONING
Take the simplest possible problem—that of choosing between
two mutually-exclusive projects A and B. There are several
ways in which this can be tackled, but the handiest criterion
is the following: Work out the present worth of each project,
using a rate of discount equal to the prescribed minimum rate
of return, and choose the project with the higher (positive)
present worth as so calculated. Take, for example, the following case:

	Project A	*Project B*
Initial Capital	2,000	4,000
Present Value of Benefits	5,300	9,480
Present Value of Costs	3,000	5,000
	2,300	4,480

Here the present worth of A is 300, and the present worth of B is 480: we should therefore choose B rather than A. This choice will maximise the total surplus of benefit over cost achievable under the given circumstances.[11]

4. PROJECTS MUTUALLY EXCLUSIVE, CAPITAL RATIONED

The rule just described for the 'no capital rationing' case will also be applicable to the capital rationing case *if* (*a*) the problem is wholly and simply that of choosing one out of a given number of mutually-exclusive projects, and *if* (*b*) there is enough capital available to allow a problem of choice between these projects to arise at all.

Normally, however, when choosing (for example) between a relatively low capital cost project A and a relatively high capital cost project B, it will first be necessary to take account of what is done with the saving of initial capital that would result from choosing A. Assuming that there are other non-mutually-exclusive projects competing for this 'saved' capital, the present worth of the best of them must be added to the present worth of A before a proper comparison with B can be made. If 'A-plus-the-other-project(s)' gives rise to a higher present worth than B, then A is to be preferred to B, and vice versa.

From this survey of the criteria which ought to be used in the four cases we have distinguished, it is evident that one of the first things the public authority concerned has to do is to select a *discount rate* for use in the calculations. All we know at this juncture about the appropriate *level* of this discount rate is that it must be equal to the prescribed minimum rate of return if present-worth-based criteria are to be capable of distinguishing between the sheep and the goats or indicating the relevant cut-off point. We cannot get round this problem by using internal-rate-of-return-based criteria, since we still have to lay down a minimum acceptable rate of return to compare with the actual internal rate of return. What considerations, then, should govern the choice of the rate of discount?

11. It will be noticed that in this case present worth per unit of initial capital investment is higher in A than in B—an indication that the uninstructed use of *rate*-of-return-based criteria in cases of this type may lead us into serious error.

This is a very important problem. For one thing, the level of the chosen rate of discount will affect the total *volume* of public investment undertaken, and therefore the relative size of the public and private sectors. The higher the rate of discount, the smaller will be the public sector relative to the private, and vice versa. And for another thing, the level of the chosen rate of discount will affect the *composition* of a given volume of public investment, since a high rate of discount discriminates against capital-intensive investments, and a low rate of discount discriminates against labour-intensive investments.[12]

The philosophy which the Government in this country adopts when selecting the rate of discount is roughly as follows. The rate must reflect, it is agreed, the minimum rate of return which is acceptable in public investment projects. And the minimum rate of return which is acceptable in *public* investment projects, it is argued, ought to be roughly the same as the minimum rate which is acceptable in *private* investment projects, after due allowance is made for differences in taxation, the degree of risk involved, and so on. Suppose it is found that the minimum rate of return which is being yielded by new investment projects in the private sector is 10% (which it is said to be at the moment). The rate of return on new projects in the public sector—and therefore the rate of discount—ought then also to be 10%. If it were less than this, the argument goes—if it were 8%, say—society would not be making the best use of its scarce resources, since there would be some resources yielding 8% in the public sector which could yield at least 10%—and therefore, impliedly, a greater surplus of benefits over costs—if they were transferred to the private sector. And if it were greater than 10%, there would be a similar kind of misallocation of resources—this time the other way round.

Whether this philosophy is a correct one or not is a matter of considerable debate. Some economists argue, for example, that one of the basic assumptions lying behind it is wrong— the assumption that the alternative to more public investment is less private investment. Might it not be less private *consumption*, or perhaps a cut in taxes? There are also grave difficulties involved in measuring the minimum acceptable

12. See the Mathematical Appendix, section 13, pp. 229–31, for an illustration of this effect.

rate of return in the private sector, and in making the proper allowances for differences in risk, etc. But until someone comes up with a formula for choosing the 'right' rate which is not only theoretically superior but also capable of translation into practical terms, it is unlikely that these criticisms will cut much ice in government circles.[13]

Finally, in order to bring our discussion down to earth a bit, let us have a brief look at an actual exercise in cost-benefit analysis—a very interesting attempt to measure the rate of return on investment in *education* in this country.[14] The Government invests a large amount of money in the provision of secondary education for 15–18-year-old pupils; and these pupils themselves also 'invest' something, in the sense that in order to receive the extra education they must forego three years' earnings. The social returns on this investment—i.e., the gains to the individuals who stay on for the extra years' schooling—can plausibly be measured by calculating the extra earnings they are likely to make during their lifetimes, over and above the earnings of those who do not stay on. The question is whether these social returns represent a high enough rate of return on the money invested.

The earnings differentials associated with the extra education were calculated to be roughly as follows:

Present Age	20–24	25–34	35–44	45–54	55–64
Earnings Differential	£195	£392	£677	£737	£765

What this means is that at the time when the survey on which this table was based was carried out (in 1964), the average earnings of people in the 20–24 age group who had stayed on were £195 higher than the average earnings of people in the same age group who had not stayed on; and so on for the other age groups in the table. It was assumed, on the basis of studies carried out in America, that about 60% of these

13. Readers who are interested in this problem will find some references in the 'Suggestions for Further Reading' at the end of this chapter.
14. What follows is based on a paper by D. Henderson-Stewart entitled 'Estimate of the Rate of Return to Education in Great Britain', which was published as an appendix to an article by M. Blaug in *The Manchester School*, September 1965.

observed differentials were directly attributable to the extra education rather than to native ability, social class, etc. It was also assumed that the total investment cost per pupil of the three years' schooling concerned was £1,500 (which includes both the outlays made by the Government and the earnings foregone by the pupils). The problem was therefore to work out the rate of return on this investment cost which 60% of the observed differentials represented.

There was one difficulty which had to be got over at the outset. The figures for the differentials in effect showed what the average differentials were at five strategic points in a lifetime. To work out the rate of return on an investment, however, as we are already aware, we have to know what the returns are in *each year*. The first job, therefore, was to make the best possible estimate, on the basis of the five average values in the table, of the pattern of the differentials between these five values. It was really the same problem of 'finding the curve which fits the dots best' which we have discussed in an earlier chapter.

The five dots in the present case are plotted in Figure 12.2.

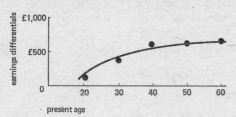

Figure 12·2

A fairly simple formula was found for a curve (also shown in the diagram) which fitted them very well indeed, namely

$$Y = 835 \left[1 - \frac{1}{(1\cdot07)^t} \right]$$

where Y = the earnings differentials, and t = time in years (equal to 1 at age 19, when the pupils concerned were assumed to begin earning). Thus the formula predicted that in the year they began earning, at age 19, the average differential would be

$$Y = 835 \left[1 - \frac{1}{(1\cdot07)^1} \right] = £55$$

In the following year, at age 20, it would be

$$Y = 835 \left[1 - \frac{1}{(1 \cdot 07)^2} \right] = £106$$

In the following year, at age 21, it would be

$$Y = 835 \left[1 - \frac{1}{(1 \cdot 07)^3} \right] = £153$$

And so on until $t = 46$, after which retirement takes place and earnings cease.

We can now readily construct the equation from which i, the internal rate of return yielded by this 'project', may be calculated. The internal rate of return, in the case of the projects we have discussed, was given by the value of i in the equation

$$\frac{B_1 - C_1}{1 + i} + \frac{B_2 - C_2}{(1 + i)^2} + \frac{B_3 - C_3}{(1 + i)^3} + \cdots \frac{B_n - C_n}{(1 + i)^n} = I$$

In the present case, single figures of differential gains take the place of the $(B - C)$'s in this equation, but the principle of the thing is precisely the same. The gains in year 1 are

$$835 \left[1 - \frac{1}{1 \cdot 07} \right]$$

so the first term in our internal rate of return equation will be

$$\frac{835 \left[1 - \frac{1}{1 \cdot 07} \right]}{1 + i}$$

The second term will be

$$\frac{835 \left[1 - \frac{1}{(1 \cdot 07)^2} \right]}{(1 + i)^2}$$

and so on for a total of 46 terms. The sum of these terms is set equal to £1,500 (the investment cost per pupil)—or, rather, to $\frac{£1,500}{0 \cdot 6}$, since it is being assumed that only 60% of the differentials are in fact directly attributable to the extra education.

All we now have to do is to solve for i, which in this case is not nearly as difficult as it looks. The result is that the internal rate of return comes out at about $12\frac{1}{2}\%$.

The author of the study I am talking about went on to make a further calculation, on a similar basis, of the rate of return on investment in *higher* education. The differentials between the earnings of those who receive higher education and the earnings of those whose education ceases between 15 and 18 seem to be roughly the same as those we have just considered. But the *cost* of higher education is very much greater, so that the internal rate of return works out appreciably lower, at about $6\frac{1}{2}\%$.[15] The combined rate for the six years of secondary and higher education taken together is about 8%.

The great problem here, of course, is whether we can have as much confidence in these rates of return on investment in education as we can in rates of return on investment in, say, electricity supply. If the rate of return on investment in the education of 15–18-year-olds is $12\frac{1}{2}\%$, whereas in higher education it is only $6\frac{1}{2}\%$, does this mean that we should give the first type of investment priority over the second, and indeed over *any* investment which yields a return of less than $12\frac{1}{2}\%$? And if the minimum acceptable rate of return is 10% (as indicated by the level of the currently prescribed rate of discount), does this mean that there should be no further investment in higher education, and that young men and women should be discouraged from going to university? Are there perhaps certain benefits (or costs) associated with university education which do not receive adequate reflection in rate of return calculations such as the one we have been considering, and if so how can we take proper account of them?

It is one of the great virtues of cost-benefit analysis that it stimulates us to ask questions like these, which are precisely those that we ought to be asking. But cost-benefit analysis has also gone at least part of the way towards providing the answers. These answers, it is true, are less clear and precise in fields like education and health than they are in electricity, water, and transport. They are less helpful when it is a question of comparing projects in two different industries like coal and steel than when it is a question of comparing a nuclear power plant and a hydro-electric plant. In its proper sphere,

15. This is, of course, the *social* rate of return. The *private* rate of return works out at about 14%.

however, cost-benefit analysis is proving itself to be of inestimable assistance in policy-making and there is no doubt that it represents an enormous improvement over the old, crude methods of assessment which it has replaced.

Suggestions for further reading

On Cost-Benefit Analysis in General:
'Cost-Benefit Analysis: A Survey', by A. R. PREST and R. TURVEY (in *Surveys of Economic Theory*, Vol. III, Macmillan, 1966)
Efficiency in Government through Systems Analysis, by R. N. MCKEAN (John Wiley & Sons, 1958)
Public Expenditure: Appraisal and Control, ed. A. T. PEACOCK and D. J. ROBERTSON (Oliver & Boyd, 1963)

On the Arithmetic of Project Appraisal:
The Capital Budgeting Decision, by H. BIERMAN and S. SMIDT (Macmillan, 2nd edn., 1966)

On the Question of the Rate of Discount:
'Investment Criteria for Public Enterprises', by P. D. HENDERSON (in *Public Enterprise: Selected Readings*, ed. R. TURVEY, Penguin Books, 1968)
Public Investment Criteria, by S. A. MARGLIN (Allen and Unwin, 1967)

On Cost-Benefit Analysis in Transport:
Transport: Selected Readings, ed. D. MUNBY (Penguin Books, 1968)

On Cost-Benefit Analysis in Education:
Economics of Education 1: Selected Readings, ed. M. BLAUG (Penguin Books, 1968)
'Estimate of the Rate of Return to Education in Great Britain', by D. HENDERSON-STEWART (appendix to an article by M. Blaug in *The Manchester School*, September, 1965)

Chapter 13
Figuring out history

In which we consider the problem of the profitability of slavery in the Southern States of America, and learn something about recent work in the field of 'Econometric History'.

Our main emphasis so far in this book has been on the use of quantitative methods in the analysis of the way in which men behave, or ought to behave, in their socio-economic relations *in present-day society*. In this final chapter, we consider the use of these methods in the analysis of the way in which men have behaved *in past society*. A number of economic historians, particularly in the United States, have in recent years been making extensive use of econometric techniques and economic models in their study of the past, and have come up with what they claim to be new facts and important reinterpretations. This 'new economic history' as its advocates call it—or 'econometric history', to use a more neutral term—has set the profession by the ears, and a book entitled *Figuring out Society* would not be complete without some reference to it.

'Econometric History' in the United States has already covered a vast field. The 'new' approach (if it is in fact 'new') has been used in studies of the role of the railroads in American history, the growth of cities, the history of banking, the development of the iron industry, the effect of tariffs on the rise of manufacturing, the economic viability of slavery, the history of cartels, and a host of other topics. In this chapter I am going to deal with only one of these studies—an article on 'The Economics of Slavery in the Antebellum South', by A. H. Conrad and J. R. Meyer—so that my treatment is going to be pretty selective. But this particular study, which was a pioneering effort in the field and has now become something of a classic, is a very typical example of the new approach,[1] and it has the additional merit of linking up rather nicely with the discussion in chapter 12 of this book.

1. Most of what follows is taken fairly directly from the article, which is republished in *Studies in Econometric History*, by A. H. Conrad and J. R. Meyer (Chapman and Hall, 1965).

The outstanding feature of agriculture in the southern states of America before the Civil War, say the authors, was its more or less exclusive reliance on slave labour. Many historians who have studied it have suggested that even without external military intervention from the north the slave economy of the south would fairly soon have toppled under its own weight. The slave system, they have argued, had in fact already reached its natural limits: it was cumbersome and economically inefficient, and would probably have destroyed itself within less than a generation.

Other historians have contested this view, however, arguing that southern plantation agriculture was at least as profitable an economic activity as most other business enterprises at that time and place. Conrad and Meyer set out to re-examine this problem by attempting, as they put it, 'to measure the profitability of southern slave operations in terms of modern capital theory'.

The great difficulty in the way of the view that slavery was profitable is the fact that there were at any rate large *parts* of the south in which agriculture was undoubtedly inefficient and unremunerative. The way in which the authors try to get over this is very ingenious. The slave economy as a whole, they argue, ought to be considered as consisting of *two* productive activities or 'industries'. First, there was the industry in which Negro slaves, together with the materials required to maintain them, were used on agricultural land to produce cotton. And second, there was the 'industry' in which the Negro slaves themselves were 'produced'—i.e., bred for sale. The authors argue that over the southern states as a whole an economically efficient system developed in which 'those regions best suited to the production of cotton (and the other important staples) specialised in agricultural production, while the less productive land continued to produce slaves, exporting the increase to the staple-crop areas'.[2]

So what the authors try to do is to calculate the expected receipts from the sale of the products of each of these two 'industries', and the expected costs involved, and to show that the excess of receipts over costs represented at least as great a return on the investment of capital as that earnable elsewhere in the economy at that time. They also attempt to show that

2. *Studies in Econometric History*, pp. 45–6.

the appropriate slave markets existed to make regional special-
isation in slave-breeding possible.

Their first task is to decide upon the way to measure the
expected profitability of investment in these two 'industries'.
The difficulty here, as we already know, is that the returns from
investment in a durable capital good—a slave, say—usually
come in only over a long period of years, so that in order to
measure profitability we have to calculate the present worth
of the project, or its internal rate of return, or both. The
present worth of a project, as we saw in chapter 12, is given
by the formula

$$\frac{B_1 - C_1}{1 + r} + \frac{B_2 - C_2}{(1 + r)^2} + \frac{B_3 - C_3}{(1 + r)^3} + \cdots \frac{B_n - C_n}{(1 + r)^n} - I$$

where B_1, B_2, etc., are the benefits (or receipts) in years 1, 2,
etc.; C_1, C_2, etc., are the operating costs in years 1, 2, etc.;
I is the initial capital investment; r is the rate of discount; and
n is the number of years of the project's life. The internal rate
of return, as we also saw in chapter 12, is given by the value
of i in the equation

$$\frac{B_1 - C_1}{1 + i} + \frac{B_2 - C_2}{(1 + i)^2} + \frac{B_3 - C_3}{(1 + i)^3} + \cdots \frac{B_n - C_n}{(1 + i)^n} = I$$

In applying these concepts to the present case, however, we
must remember that we are now seeking to calculate *private*,
and not social, returns—i.e., the returns that the owners of
plantations will expect to receive on their investment, without
any reference whatever to the *social* benefits and costs which
may be involved. This means that the benefits (or receipts)
and costs which we list in our balance-sheet will be pretty
much the same as those which the plantation owner himself
would have listed in his.

What *rate of discount* ought we to use in our calculations of
present worth in this case? Presumably we ought to use a rate
of discount which reflects the best rate of return the plantation
owner could have got if he had put the capital concerned to
one of its other possible uses. If we did this, and if the present
worth of a plantation investment project then came out as
greater than zero (or, what amounts to the same thing, if the

so-called 'benefit-cost ratio' came out as greater than 1),[3] we could interpret this result as meaning that the plantation owner would have regarded the project as relatively profitable in comparison with other possible uses of his capital. The difficulty is that what the owner in fact regarded as other possible uses of his capital may have differed quite widely according to the circumstances in which he was placed, or in which he conceived himself as being placed. This is a problem to which Conrad and Meyer give too little attention. But since they in fact do three separate calculations using three different rates of discount—4%, 6%, and 8%—and since it seems very likely that the relevant rate lay somewhere within this range, we are perhaps justified in forgetting about this problem.

Having dealt with—or side-stepped—this tricky point, the next job is to derive actual real-life figures to put on the unknowns in the present worth formula, first in the case of the industry producing the final good (cotton), and then in the case of the industry producing the intermediate good (slaves).

In the first industry, the basic initial investment is in the slave, plus the appurtenant land; and the average length of the project will correspond to the average length of life of a slave. From such figures as are available, the authors calculate that the average life-expectancy of 20-year-old Negroes working as prime cotton hands on southern plantations in 1830–35 was about 30–35 years, so in most of their calculations they take n as $= 30$.

Now for I, the cost of the initial capital investment. Slave prices for prime field hands in the period concerned apparently ranged around an average of something like $1,000. The amount of land employed per field hand was anything from 15 to 35 acres, costing an average of something like $450. Putting these capital costs together with the costs of ploughs, wagons, cabins, etc., the authors calculate that the *total* investment per male slave averaged about $1,400–$1,450, the range running from about $1,250 to $1,650.[4]

3. The 'benefit-cost ratio' is here defined as the ratio of the sum of the discounted $(B - C)$'s to the initial capital I. If this ratio works out as >1, it follows that the present worth of the project is >0. The amount by which the ratio exceeds 1 measures the present worth per unit of initial capital investment, as defined in chapter 12.

4. *Studies in Econometric History*, pp. 50–53.

There remain for valuation the $(B-C)$'s—i.e., the receipts operating costs involved in the production process. In the case of the first industry (as distinct from the second), these are worked out on an annual average basis, so that they are assumed to be the same for each of the 30 years of the investment. This greatly simplifies the calculation of the present value of the stream of $(B-C)$'s, since we can find this very simply from annuity tables.[5]

So far as receipts are concerned, the number of bales of cotton per field hand per year apparently varied from about 3 on the poorest land to about 7 on the best land. Each bale contained 400 lb., and the realised farm price of cotton (i.e., the export price minus marketing costs) averaged about 7–9 cents per lb. On the costs side, the maintenance of a slave for a year cost about $20–$21.

The calculations made by the authors on the basis of these figures are set out in Table 13.1. Cases 1, 2, and 3 represent the most typical situation, where the capital outlay per hand was $1,350–£1,400, and the average yield of cotton per hand was about $3\frac{3}{4}$ bales per annum. The calculation is done in these and all the other cases for three different prices of cotton (7, 8, and 9 cents per lb.), and at three different rates of discount (4%, 6%, and 8%). Cases 4, 5, and 6 represent the situation on rather better land, the capital outlay per hand being somewhat higher ($1,600), and the yield per hand also being higher ($4\frac{1}{2}$ bales). Cases 7, 8, and 9 represent what the authors call 'the minimum of profitability, or what might be expected on poor upland pine country or the worked-out lands of the eastern seaboard'. Here the capital outlay is lower ($1,250–$1,300), but so is the yield per hand (3 bales). Finally, cases 10, 11, and 12 show the upper range of profitability. The capital outlay is relatively high ($1,700), but so is the yield per hand (7 bales). In each case a calculation is also made of the relevant internal rate of return.

To illustrate the method of calculation employed, take case 6, where the capital outlay is $1,600. The annual farm receipts

5. Annuity tables tell us (*inter alia*) what sum we would have to pay now in order to buy ourselves an annual income of some given amount (x) for a given number of years (n) at a given rate of interest (r). In other words, they tell us the *present value* of an annuity of x for n years at a rate of discount of r.

Table 13.1

Realised Returns on Prime Field Hands Under Various Hypothesised Conditions

Case	Capital Outlay per Hand	Yield per Hand (Bales)	Average Net Farm Price (Cents)	Benefit/Cost Ratios at 4%	at 6%	at 8%	Approximate Internal Rate of Return (%)
1	$1,350–$1,400	3¾	7	1·07	0·85	0·70	4·5
2	$1,350–$1,400	3¾	8	1·26	1·00	0·82	5·2
3	$1,350–$1,400	3¾	9	1·45	1·15	0·94	6·5
4	$1,600	4½	7	1·15	0·91	0·74	5·0
5	$1,600	4½	8	1·34	1·07	0·87	7·0
6	$1,600	4½	9	1·54	1·22	1·00	8·0
7	$1,250–$1,300	3	7	0·87	0·69	0·55	2·2
8	$1,250–$1,300	3	8	1·00	0·82	0·67	3·9
9	$1,250–$1,300	3	9	1·19	0·95	0·78	5·4
10	$1,700	7	7	1·79	1·43	1·16	10·0
11	$1,700	7	8	2·03	1·65	1·35	12·0
12	$1,700	7	9	2·35	1·88	1·53	13·0

per hand, in cents, are $4\frac{1}{2}$ (the number of bales produced per hand per year) multiplied by 400 (the number of lb. in a bale) multiplied by 9 (the price in cents per lb.). They are thus $4\frac{1}{2} \times 400 \times 9 = 16,200$ cents $= \$162$. The costs of maintenance of the slave we assume to be $20 per annum, so that the value of $(B - C)$ for each of the 30 years of the investment will be $162 - $20 = 142. We now calculate the present value of this 30-year stream of $(B - C)$'s at a discount rate of, say, 6% per annum. Looking up an annuity table, we find that the present value of an annuity of $142 for 30 years at a discount rate of 4% is $1,954·6. Thus the present worth of the investment is $1,954·6 - $1,600 = $354·6. The benefit-cost ratio is $\frac{1,954·6}{1,600} = 1·22$, and the present worth per unit of capital investment is $\frac{354·6}{1,600} = 0·22$, or 22%.[6]

If the figures on which these calculations are based are accurate, the overall 'profitability' (in the relevant sense) of these operations is clearly indicated by the table. In the first six cases, which according to the authors encompass the majority of antebellum cotton plantation operations, the benefit-cost ratio is almost always above unity at discount rates of 4% and 6%; and the internal rate of return only once falls below 5% and in case 6 rises as high as 8%. Cases 10, 11, and 12, representing operations on the best land, are highly profitable under all the hypothesised circumstances. It is only cases 7, 8, and 9, representing operations on the worst land, that appear relatively 'unprofitable': here the plantation owner would do badly, *unless he could supplement his income by breeding slaves.*

Let us turn, then, to the similar—but more complex—calculations made by Conrad and Meyer of the profitability of the second 'industry', that in which slaves were bred for sale. The investment here is in a *female* slave, who is assumed to be of benefit to her owner not only by virtue of the field work she performs, but also by virtue of (*a*) the field work performed by her children in their early years, and (*b*) the price realised for her children when they are sold. This means

6. It is not nearly so easy to work out the internal rate of return, the authors' approximate figures for which (in each of the twelve cases) are given in the final column of the table.

that the receipts side of the balance-sheet is more complicated than in the case of the first industry. And the costs side, too, is more complicated, since account has to be taken of the costs of maintaining the children and the nursery costs associated with their births.

The authors calculate receipts and costs over the assumed lifetime of a slave who bears five children during her life, and a slave who bears ten, these being apparently the actual lower

Table 13.2

Annual returns on a prime field wench investment (working on land which yielded 3·75 bales per prime male field hand, assuming a 7½ cent net farm price for cotton and ten 'salable' children born to every wench)

Year from Purchase Date	Personal Field Returns	Child Field Returns	Child Sale Returns	Personal Upkeep	Child Upkeep	Net Returns
1	$56	—	—	$20	—	$36
2	40	—	—	20	$50	−30
3	56	—	—	20	10	26
4	40	—	—	20	60	−40
5	56	—	—	20	20	16
6	40	—	—	20	70	−50
7	56	—	—	20	30	6
8	40	$3·75	—	20	80	−56·25
9	56	7·50	—	20	45	−1·50
10	40	15·00	—	20	95	−50·00
11	56	22·50	—	20	60	−1·50
12	40	37·50	—	20	110	−52·50
13	56	52·50	—	20	75	13·50
14	40	75·00	—	20	120	−35·00
15	56	97·50	—	20	95	47·50
16	40	127·50	—	20	150	−2·50
17	56	157·50	—	20	115	78·50
18	40	195·00	—	20	165	55·00
19	56	232·50	—	20	130	134·30
20	40	195·00	$875	20	170	920·00
21	56	232·50	—	20	130	138·50
22	56	195·00	875	20	120	986·00
23	56	232·50	—	20	120	148·50
24	56	195·00	875	20	110	996·00
25	56	232·50	—	20	110	158·00
26	56	195·00	875	20	100	1,006·00
27	56	232·50	—	20	100	168·00
28	56	187·50	875	20	90	1,008·50
29	56	225·00	—	20	90	171·00
30	56	180·00	875	20	80	1,011·00
31	—	210·00	—	—	80	130·00
32	—	157·50	875	—	60	972·50
33	—	180·00	—	—	60	120·00
34	—	120·00	875	—	40	955·00
35	—	135·00	—	—	40	95·00
36	—	67·50	875	—	20	922·50
37	—	75·00	—	—	20	55·00
38	—	—	875	—	—	875·00

and upper limits. The calculations for the ten-children case are set out in Table 13.2. It is assumed that successful pregnancies are spaced two years apart, the first occurring in the second year from the purchase date. The slave's personal field returns are assumed to be $56 in the years when she is not pregnant, and $40 in the years when she is (see the column headed 'Personal Field Returns'). The expenses of her personal upkeep are assumed to be $20 in each year of her life (see the column headed 'Personal Upkeep'). The assumptions made about the children will be clarified as we go through the table step by step.

In the first year after the purchase date the slave is not pregnant, so her personal field returns are $56. Thus after $20 is paid out for her personal upkeep, her owner receives a net return of $36 (see last column). In the second year she is pregnant, so her personal field returns are $40. Her personal upkeep is $20, but nursery costs in respect of her first child (assumed to be $50 per successful pregnancy) have to be paid (see the column headed 'Child Upkeep'). Thus the net return is $40 − ($20 + $50), i.e., a *negative* return of −$30. In the third year she is not pregnant, so her personal field returns are $56. Her personal upkeep is $20, and in addition her child has to be maintained, at a cost assumed to be $10 per year for children between one and six, $15 per year for 7 to 12-year-olds, and $20 per year (the full adult maintenance cost) for those aged 13 and over. In the third year, therefore, the net return is $56 − ($20 + $10) = $26.

In the fourth year she is again pregnant, so her personal field returns are $40; her personal upkeep is $20; the nursery costs in respect of her second child are $50; and the upkeep of her first child costs $10. The net return is therefore $40 − ($20 + $50 + $10) = −$40. In the fifth year she is not pregnant, so her personal field returns are $56; her personal upkeep is $20; and the upkeep of her first and second children is $20. The net return is therefore $56 − ($20 + $20) = $16. In the sixth year she is pregnant, so her personal field returns are $40; her personal upkeep is $20; the nursery costs in respect of her third child are $50; and the upkeep of her first and second children is $20. The net return is therefore $40 − ($20 + $50 + $20) = −$50.

Skipping the seventh year, we come to the eighth, in which her first child, now aged 6, starts working in the fields, so that the field returns of the child have now to be taken into account. A set of assumptions about the value of these returns, and the way in which they increase from year to year until the child is sold at age 18, is made for both male and female children, and these assumptions are reflected in the year-by-year figures in the column headed 'Child Field Returns'. In the eighth year, then, the slave is pregnant, so her personal field returns are $40; her first child's field returns are $3·75; her personal upkeep is $20; nursery costs in respect of her fourth child are $50; and the upkeep of her first, second, and third children is $30. The net return is therefore $40 + $3·75 − ($20 + $80) = −$56·25.

The progression goes on in this orderly way until the twentieth year, when her first child, now aged 18, is sold, at an assumed purchase price of $875. In the twentieth year the slave is pregnant with her tenth and last child, so that her personal field returns are $40; the field returns of those of her children aged 6 and over who are working in the fields now total $195; the proceeds from the sale of her first child are $875; her personal upkeep is $20; the nursery costs in respect of her tenth child are $50; and the maintenance costs in respect of her other nine children now total $120. Thus the net returns are $40 + $195 + $875 − ($20 + $170) = $920.

The slave goes on working for another ten years, when she is assumed to die, and her personal field returns and personal upkeep cease abruptly. Her children are successively sold when they reach the age of 18, so that child field returns and child upkeep eventually decline. When the tenth child is sold, in the thirty-eighth year after the purchase of the slave, this incredibly sad and sordid story is brought to a close with a last net return of $875 to the investor.

The final task for our authors is to calculate, on the basis of the stream of net returns listed in the last column of the table (and an assumed initial investment of $1,200–$1,300 in the slave, the appurtenant land, and the equipment) the benefit-cost ratio and internal rate of return associated with this investment. In the case we have just considered, where the mother bears ten children, a benefit-cost ratio of 1·62 (at a discount rate of 6%) is yielded, and an internal rate of return of 8·1%. In the other case which the authors analyse, where the mother is assumed to bear only five children, the benefit-cost ratio works out at 1·23, and the internal rate of return at

7·1%. These returns, it will be seen, are somewhat higher than those prevailing in the first industry.

If the authors are right, then, the expectation at the time was that investment in slavery, by and large, would be at least as remunerative as the other alternative employments to which the capital might have been put. Cotton growing gave really *large* returns, it is true, only on the best land, but a general sharing in prosperity could be guaranteed if slaves could be bred and reared on the worst land and then sold to those owning the best.[7]

Could they, though? Is there any evidence of the existence of a slave *market*, through which slaves could be expeditiously and economically transferred from the regions where the land was bad, but which could profitably specialise in slave-breeding, to the regions where the land was good, and where cotton-growing by slave labour was therefore profitable?

If a slave market of this kind did exist, the authors argue, and if slave-breeding was in fact profitable, one would expect to find evidence of this in the *prices* of female slaves. A very ingenious comparison is made by the authors at this stage in their argument. Table 13.3 shows the annual *hiring* rates for male and female slaves, which must evidently reflect the market's valuation of the relative productivity of males and females *in work in the fields*. Now if female slaves were in fact purchased for breeding purposes, and if this was profitable, and if there was a market in female slaves, we ought to find that the price differentials as between males and females were less in the case of *purchase* prices than they were in the case of *hiring* prices. And if the figures in Table 13.4 are to be believed, this is precisely what we do find. In every case but one, the purchase price differential is narrower than the hiring rate differential.

And so the authors reach their general conclusion. 'In sum' they say, 'it seems doubtful that the South was forced by bad statesmanship into an unnecessary war to protect a system that must soon have disappeared because it was economically unsound. This is a romantic hypothesis, which will not stand against the facts.'[8]

What are we to say about this remarkable exercise in

7. *Studies in Econometric History*, p. 66.
8. *Ibid.*, p. 82.

'econometric history'—and about 'econometric history' in general? First let us look at what Professor Conrad himself said about it, in a paper[9] written some ten years after the

Table 13.3

Annual Hiring Rates for Male and Female
Slaves (Including Rations and Clothing),
by States, 1860

State	Men	Women	Ratio (Men: Women)
Virginia	$105	$46	2·28
North Carolina	110	49	2·25
South Carolina	103	55	1·87
Georgia	124	75	1·65
Florida	139	80	1·74
Alabama	138	89	1·55
Mississippi	166	100	1·66
Louisiana	171	120	1·43
Texas	166	109	1·52
Arkansas	170	108	1·57
Tennessee	121	63	1·92

original article by himself and J. R. Meyer. 'What we did,' he wrote, 'was to imagine twelve typical southern plantations all growing cotton, but with four different land qualities, represented by the average yield per hand, each facing a range of three different farm-gate prices. Then, using this statistical model, implemented or quantified as best we could with data from contemporary reports and secondary sources, we derived an answer to the following question: Should a Southerner, purchasing land and slaves in the mid-'forties, have expected to make a return on his investment that was at least comparable to what was then being earned on other long-term investments? The answer was *yes*. . . . The question as we framed it was evidently a strange one for historians to raise. We could not ask whether investments made in 1845, say, were *in fact* profitable, since Emancipation intervened

9. 'Econometrics and Southern History', by A. H. Conrad (reprinted in *The New Economic History: Recent Papers on Methodology*, ed. R. L. Andreano, John Wiley & Sons, 1970).

Table 13.4

Selected Prices of Male and Female Slaves, 1859 and 1860

State (Year)	Age	Condition	Male Price	Female Price	Ratio
Virginia (1859)	17–20	Best	$1,350–$1,425	$1,275–$1,325	1·07
South Carolina	—	Prime Wench	$1,325	$1,283	1·03
South Carolina (1859)	—	Field Hand	$1,555	$1,705	0·91
Georgia	21	Girl	$1,900	—	0·88
	17	Best field hand (9 mo. inf.)	—	[$2,150]	
Georgia (1859)	—	Prime, young	$1,300	—	1·04
	—	Cotton hand, house servant	—	$1,250	
Alabama (1859)	19	—	$1,635	—	1·37
	18, 18, 8	—	—	$1,193	1·12
Mississippi	—	No. 1 field hand	$1,625	$1,450	
Texas	21, 15	—	$2,015	$1,635	1·23
Texas (1859)	17, 14	—	$1,527	$1,403	1·09

and wiped out the slave-holders' property-rights, long before the economic life of the prime field hand or wench purchased in the mid-'forties had been realised. Nor did we look for plantation records to evaluate, as other historians have done, either believing them to be representative, or with a view to combining their earnings experience to get some kind of average for the South. It was our question, then, and the capital model implied in it, that prompted Fritz Redlich to deny us the proud title of professional historian and to label us, instead, as quasi-historians. . . . What this piece of econometrics contributed was, evidently, not a new observation about the course of southern history, but rather a new way of approaching the problem.'[10]

So the 'new economic history' represents much more than a concern with numbers. Almost *all* economic historians have been concerned, at any rate up to a point, with quantifying the economic magnitudes which interest them, and if mere quantification were the hallmark of the distinction between the 'old' and the 'new', then 'econometric history' could hardly claim to represent a revolution. What is said to be new and distinctive 'is not simply measurement but a redirection of quantification in ways that reconstruct economic data which might have existed but are not now available, and in making measurements that were never before made'. As Professor R. W. Fogel has put it, 'It seems clear that what is most novel and most important in the New Economic History is not the increased emphasis on measurement but the reliance on theory to measure that which was previously deemed un-measurable'.[11]

One should not, however, exaggerate the newness of even *this* 'new' feature. The things which 'econometric history' actually does do not seem to me to be very different, in essence, from those which many contemporary economic historians do, and which most of them have always done in the past. There is a difference in *emphasis*, it is true; a difference in the *sources* which are concentrated upon; and a difference in the *language* which is used—the new jargon of econometrics is employed in the context of the old problems. And I have no doubt that

10. *The New Economic History*, pp. 114–15.
11. I have taken both these quotations from the editor's introduction to *New Views on American Economic Development*, ed. R. L. Andreano (Schenkman Publishing Co., 1965), pp. 4–5.

some of the tendencies in the 'old' history against which the 'new' historians are reacting did deserve to be reacted against —e.g., an apparent lack of concern in some quarters with the vital problems of explanation and causality, and a tendency to claim that economic history has little to learn from economics. But when we think about it, we see that there is nothing really new about the use of models and equations in economic history. All historians, and not merely economic historians, *in effect* use equations, whether they are aware of it or not, and whether or not they put actual figures on the parameters of the equations. As the reader of this book must know by now, whenever we say that something is associated with, or depends upon, or is caused by something else, we are in effect putting the relationship between the variables in 'equational' form—even if only in the very general form $y = f(x)$. Professor Fogel, perhaps the shrewdest of the 'new' economic historians, has made this point very effectively. 'If the ubiquity of mathematics in history is not more widely recognised,' he says, 'it is because the equations of literary historians are usually camouflaged by words. The camouflage frequently hides the fact that what is often posed as debate regarding the legitimacy of mathematics in history is really a disagreement about the values of the parameters of equations that have, at least implicitly, been employed by all of the disputants.'[12]

Similarly, when Conrad refers to the application of economic models to history, to their testing, and to the econometric problem of identification which arises in this testing, he is not really asking for much more than the *conscious* and *explicit* use of techniques which up to a point have always been *un*consciously or *im*plicitly employed in economic history. In essence, what he is saying is that the explicit formulation of problems in terms of modern economic theory, and the explicit use of modern quantitative techniques, will often help to throw further light on these problems.

But why, the reader may be asking, this more or less exclusive concentration by the 'new' economic historians on *economic* theory and *economic* models? The most obvious answer, I suppose, is that if we are going to use models at all in *economic* history, it is *economic* models which are likely to be most useful. But I wonder whether there may not be a little

12. *The New Economic History*, p. 131.

more to it than this? Many economic historians in the United States, when training for their profession, learn a lot about economics and econometric techniques. Not nearly so many of them learn anything much about psychology, sociology, and politics, and the new models and techniques of analysis which these sciences are developing. Yet it may be that in relation at any rate to *some* problems of economic history, these other sciences have just as much to offer as economics.[13] Maybe another 'revolution' in economic history is just around the corner!

While we are waiting for it, however, let us pause to salute the very substantial contribution to the understanding of society and its development which the 'econometric history' of the past ten or fifteen years has made. Once again the great power of modern quantitative methods, and the way in which their use may stimulate us to ask—and up to a point to answer—extremely interesting and relevant questions, have been abundantly demonstrated.

13. Cf. *The New Economic History*, pp. 146–50.

Suggestions for further reading

On the Profitability of the Slave Economy:
　Studies in Econometric History, by A. H. CONRAD and J. R. MEYER
　(Chapman and Hall, 1965)

On 'Econometric History' in General:
　New Views on American Economic Development, ed. R. L. ANDREANO (Schenkman Publishing Co., 1965)
　Essays in American Economic History, ed. A. W. COATS and R. M. ROBERTSON (Edward Arnold, 1969)
　The New Economic History: Recent Papers on Methodology, ed. R. L. ANDREANO (John Wiley & Sons, 1970)

Mathematical Appendix

1. *Some Conventional Signs and Modes of Expression*

$a = b$ a is equal to b, or the same as b

$a \neq b$ a is not equal to b

$a > b$ a is greater than b

$a < b$ a is less than b

$a \geq b$ a is greater than or equal to b (i.e., not less than b)

$a \leq b$ a is less than or equal to b (i.e., not greater than b)

$\left.\begin{array}{l} ab \\ a \cdot b \\ a \times b \end{array}\right\}$ a multiplied by b

$\left.\begin{array}{l} a(b + c) \\ a \cdot (b + c) \\ a \times (b + c) \end{array}\right\}$ a multiplied by the sum of b and c

$\left.\begin{array}{l} a\dfrac{b}{c} \\ a \cdot \dfrac{b}{c} \\ a \times \dfrac{b}{c} \end{array}\right\}$ a multiplied by the quotient obtained when b is divided by c

a^b a raised to the power of b (i.e., $a \times a \times a \times a \times \ldots$ to b factors)

$\sqrt{a}$ the square root of a (i.e., the number which, when multiplied by itself, will yield a)

$\sqrt[b]{a}$ The bth root of a (i.e., the number which, when raised to the power of b, will yield a)

2. *Some Rules of Algebra*[1]

(i) Adding a negative number $(-a)$ is the same as subtracting a positive number a. *Illustrations:*
$$b + (-a) = b - a$$
$$3 + (-2) = 3 - 2 = 1$$

(ii) Subtracting a negative number $(-a)$ is the same as adding a positive number a. *Illustrations:*
$$b - (-a) = b + a$$
$$3 - (-2) = 3 + 2 = 5$$

(iii) When any number is multiplied by 0 the product is 0. *Illustrations:*
$$a \times 0 = 0$$
$$15 \times 0 = 0$$

(iv) The product of a positive number a and a negative number $(-b)$ is $-ab$. *Illustrations:*
$$a(-b) = -ab$$
$$7(-3) = -(7 \times 3) = -21$$

(v) The product of two negative numbers $(-a)$ and $(-b)$ is ab. *Illustrations:*
$$(-a)(-b) = ab$$
$$(-8)(-5) = 40$$

(vi) If a positive number a is raised to the power of b, the result is always a positive number. If a negative number $(-a)$ is raised to the power of b, the result is a positive number when b is even and a negative number when b is odd. *Illustrations:*

$$a \times a \times a \times \ldots \text{ to } b \text{ factors} = a^b$$
$$a \times a = a^2$$
$$a \times a \times a = a^3$$
$$(-a) \times (-a) = a^2$$
$$(-a) \times (-a) \times (-a) = -a^3$$
$$(-3)^2 = 9$$
$$(-3)^3 = -27$$

(vii) If a single bracket is preceded by a positive sign, the bracket may be removed without changing the signs of the terms within it. *Illustrations:*
$$+(a - b + c - d) = a - b + c - d$$
$$+(6 - 2 + 4 - 1) = 6 - 2 + 4 - 1 = 7$$

1. In this and the two following sections, the ' $=$ ' sign means 'is the same as' or 'is identical to'.

(viii) If a single bracket is preceded by a negative sign, the bracket may be removed if the signs of the terms within it are all changed. *Illustrations:*
$$- (a - b + c - d) = -a + b - c + d$$
$$- (6 - 2 + 4 - 1) = -6 + 2 - 4 + 1 = -7$$

3. *Some Rules About Fractions*

(i) Addition of fractions:
$$\frac{a}{b} + \frac{c}{d} = \frac{ad + bc}{bd}$$
$$\frac{3}{4} + \frac{2}{5} = \frac{15 + 8}{4 \times 5} = \frac{23}{20} = 1\frac{3}{20}$$

(ii) Subtraction of fractions:
$$\frac{a}{b} - \frac{c}{d} = \frac{ad - bc}{bd}$$
$$\frac{3}{4} - \frac{2}{5} = \frac{15 - 8}{4 \times 5} = \frac{7}{20}$$

(iii) Multiplication of fractions:
$$\frac{a}{b} \cdot \frac{c}{d} = \frac{ac}{bd}$$
$$\frac{3}{4} \cdot \frac{2}{5} = \frac{3 \times 2}{4 \times 5} = \frac{6}{20} = \frac{3}{10}$$

(iv) Division of fractions:
$$\frac{a}{b} \div \frac{c}{d} = \frac{a}{b} \cdot \frac{d}{c} = \frac{ad}{bc}$$
$$\frac{3}{4} \div \frac{2}{5} = \frac{3}{4} \cdot \frac{5}{2} = \frac{15}{8} = 1\frac{7}{8}$$

(v) Signs of fractions:
$$\frac{-a}{b} = \frac{a}{-b} = -\frac{a}{b}$$
$$\frac{-3}{4} = \frac{3}{-4} = -\frac{3}{4}$$
$$\frac{-a}{-b} = \frac{a}{b}$$
$$\frac{-3}{-4} = \frac{3}{4}$$

4. *Some Rules about Powers*

(i) $a^m a^n = a^{m+n}$. *Illustration:*

$$2^3 \cdot 2^4 = (2 \times 2 \times 2)(2 \times 2 \times 2 \times 2)$$
$$= 2^7 = 3^{3+4}$$

(ii) $(a^m)^n = a^{mn}$. *Illustration:*

$$(2^3)^2 = (2 \times 2 \times 2)(2 \times 2 \times 2)$$
$$= 2^6 = 2^{3 \times 2}$$

(iii) $\left(\dfrac{a}{b}\right)^n = \dfrac{a^n}{b^n}$. *Illustration:*

$$\left(\frac{2}{3}\right)^4 = \frac{2}{3} \times \frac{2}{3} \times \frac{2}{3} \times \frac{2}{3}$$

$$= \frac{2 \times 2 \times 2 \times 2}{3 \times 3 \times 3 \times 3} = \frac{2^4}{3^4}$$

(iv) $\dfrac{a^m}{a^n} = a^{m-n}$ (when $m > n$). *Illustration:*

$$\frac{2^5}{2^3} = \frac{2 \times 2 \times 2 \times 2 \times 2}{2 \times 2 \times 2}$$

$$= 2^2 = 2^{5-3}$$

(v) $\dfrac{a^m}{a^n} = \dfrac{1}{a^{n-m}}$ (when $m < n$). *Illustration:*

$$\frac{2^4}{2^6} = \frac{2 \times 2 \times 2 \times 2}{2 \times 2 \times 2 \times 2 \times 2 \times 2}$$

$$= \frac{1}{2^2} = \frac{1}{2^{6-4}}$$

N.B. The above rules apply only when the indices concerned, m and n, are positive whole numbers. When they are not positive whole numbers—i.e., when they are zero, or negative, or fractions—they are defined as obeying rule (i) above, i.e.

$$a^m a^n = a^{m+n}$$

for all values of m and n. The following rules set out the meanings of a^0, a^{-m}, and $a^{1/m}$ to which we are led by this definition.

(vi) $a^0 = 1$ (if $a \neq 0$). *Proof:*
By rule (i), $a^0 a^m = a^{0+m} = a^m$
Dividing both sides by a^m,

$$a^0 = \frac{a^m}{a^m} = 1$$

(vii) $a^{-m} = \dfrac{1}{a^m}$ (if $a \neq 0$). *Proof:*

By rule (i), $a^{-m}a^m = a^{-m+m} = a^0 = 1$

Dividing both sides by a^m,

$$a^{-m} = \frac{1}{a^m}$$

(viii) $a^{1/m} = \sqrt[m]{a}$. *Proof:*

By rule (i), $a^{1/m} \times a^{1/m} \times a^{1/m} \times \ldots$ to m factors
$$= a^{m(1/m)}$$
$$= a^{m/m} = a$$

Taking the mth root of both sides,
$$a^{1/m} = \sqrt[m]{a}$$

5. *Some Rules about the Manipulation of Equations*[2]

(i) A term may be moved from one side to the other, provided the sign in front of it is altered. *Illustration:*

If $\qquad 2x - 5 = 17$
then $\qquad 2x = 17 + 5$

(ii) The same number may be added to each side. *Illustration:*

If $\qquad 3x + 4 = 22$
then $\quad 3x + 4 + 6 = 22 + 6$

(iii) The same number may be subtracted from each side. *Illustration:*

If $\qquad 3x + 4 = 22$
then $\quad 3x + 4 - 6 = 22 - 6$

(iv) Each side may be multiplied by the same number. *Illustration:*

If $\qquad 4x - 5 = 31$
then $\qquad 2(4x - 5) = 2(31)$

(v) Each side may be divided by the same number. *Illustration:*

If $\qquad 4x - 5 = 31$
then $\qquad \dfrac{4x - 5}{3} = \dfrac{31}{3}$

2. In this and the two following sections, the ' $=$ ' sign in the equations means that there is some value for x which will *make* the two sides equal.

(vi) Each side may be raised to the same power. *Illustration:*

If $\qquad 3x + 2 = 20$

then $\qquad (3x + 2)^3 = 20^3$

(vii) The same root may be taken of each side. *Illustration:*

If $\qquad 4x - 5 = 7,$

then $\sqrt[4]{4x - 5} = \sqrt[4]{7}$

6. *Two Examples of the Solution of Simple Equations by Manipulation*

(i) $\qquad\qquad\qquad 2x + \dfrac{x}{3} = 2\tfrac{1}{2} - 5x$

Multiply each side by 3.

$$3\left(2x + \frac{x}{3}\right) = 3(2\tfrac{1}{2} - 5x)$$

Multiply out. $\qquad 6x + x = 7\tfrac{1}{2} - 15x$

$\qquad\qquad \therefore \qquad 7x = 7\tfrac{1}{2} - 15x$

Move last term to left-hand side.

$$7x + 15x = 7\tfrac{1}{2}$$
$$\therefore \qquad 22x = 7\tfrac{1}{2}$$

Divide each side by 22.

$$\frac{22x}{22} = \frac{7\tfrac{1}{2}}{22}$$

$$\therefore \qquad x = \frac{7\tfrac{1}{2}}{22} = \frac{15}{44}$$

(ii) $\qquad\qquad\qquad \dfrac{3x^3 - 2x^2}{4} = 6 - \dfrac{x^2}{2}$

Multiply each side by 4.

$$3x^3 - 2x^2 = 24 - 2x^2$$

Move last term to left-hand side.

$$3x^3 - 2x^2 + 2x^2 = 24$$
$$\therefore \qquad 3x^3 = 24$$

Divide each side by 3.
$$x^3 = 8$$
Take cube root of each side.
$$x = \sqrt[3]{8} = 2$$

7. *Two Examples of the Solution of Simultaneous Equations*

(i) Suppose we have a system of two equations, such that

$$x + y = 21 \quad . \quad . \quad . \quad . \quad . \quad . \quad . \quad . \quad (1)$$
$$x - y = 3 \quad . \quad . \quad . \quad . \quad . \quad . \quad . \quad . \quad (2)$$

We can find values for x and y which will satisfy both these equations by subtracting equation (2) from equation (1):

$$x + y = 21$$
$$x - y = 3$$
$$\overline{}$$
$$2y = 18$$

Thus $y = 9$, and if we substitute this value for y in either of the two equations we immediately find that $x = 12$.

Alternatively, we could have written equation (1) as
$$x = 21 - y$$
and substituted this for x in equation (2):
$$(21 - y) - y = 3$$
$$21 - 2y = 3$$
$$2y = 18$$
$$y = 9, \text{ and } x = 12$$

(ii) Suppose now that we have a system of the two following equations:

$$5x - 3y = 34 \quad . \quad . \quad . \quad . \quad . \quad . \quad . \quad (1)$$
$$3x - 4y = 16 \quad . \quad . \quad . \quad . \quad . \quad . \quad . \quad (2)$$

Subtraction of one of these equations from the other, at any rate as they stand, will not help us to obtain a solution, since the coefficients of both x and y in the first equation are different from their coefficients in the second. We can make the coefficients of one of the unknowns the same, however, by suitable multiplication of the equations. Various ways of doing this are possible. Suppose, for example, that we multiply equation (1) by 4, and equation (2) by 3. Equation (1) then becomes $20x - 12y = 136$, and equation (2) then becomes $9x - 12y = 48$. The coefficient of y is now -12 in both equations, so that if we subtract the second from the first y will be eliminated:[3]

$$\begin{array}{r} 20x - 12y = 136 \\ 9x - 12y = 48 \\ \hline 11x = 88 \end{array}$$

Thus $x = 8$, and if we substitute this value for x in either of the two equations we immediately find that $y = 2$.

Alternatively, we could have written equation (1) as

$$x = \frac{34 + 3y}{5}$$

and substituted this for x in equation (2):

$$3\left(\frac{34 + 3y}{5}\right) - 4y = 16$$
$$3(34 + 3y) - 20y = 80$$
$$102 + 9y - 20y = 80$$
$$11y = 22$$
$$y = 2, \text{ and } x = 8$$

8. *The Concept of a Function*

In the social sciences, we are very often concerned with certain measurable quantities like the price of petrol, the number of suicides per annum, the output of pig iron, the birth rate, the level of employment, etc., the magnitude of which may *vary* over a range of possible values. The *relations of dependence* which exist or may exist between the values of selected variables of this type constitute one of the main fields of inquiry in the social sciences.

When the values of two variables do not move independently of one another, and the nature of the relation between them is such that when the value of one of them is known the value or values that the other can take are fixed and determined, we say that there is a *functional relation* between them. If we are looking at this relation from the

3. If the signs of the coefficient were different, *addition* of the two equations, and not subtraction, would eliminate y.

angle of the dependence of the values of one (specific) variable upon those of the other, we often separate the two variables into a *dependent* variable (usually symbolised by y) and an *independent* variable (usually symbolised by x), and speak of the first variable as a *function* of the second.

If we want merely to express the fact that a dependent variable y is a function of an independent variable x, without stating the specific *form* of the function, we normally write

$$y = f(x), \text{ read as '}y \text{ is a function of } x\text{'}$$

[*N.B.* '$f(x)$' does *not* mean 'f multiplied by x']

If we *do* wish to state the specific form of the function, we first fix on the units in which y and x are to be measured, and then express the relationship between the two variables in algebraic form, in such a way that if the value of x is known the value of y can be deduced from it.

Suppose, for example, that there is a functional relationship between the demand for apples by households in a particular town (here regarded as the dependent variable) and the price of apples (here regarded as the independent variable), and that the form of the function is such that the number of tons of apples demanded per month is equal to 40 minus (3 times the price of apples in pence per pound). We then write

$$y = f(x) = 40 - 3x$$

From this, knowing what x and y stand for and the units in which they are being measured, we can immediately determine, for any given value of x, the corresponding value of y. If $x = 3$ pence, for example, $y = 31$ tons. If $x = 4$, $y = 28$; if $x = 5$, $y = 25$; and so on.

9. *Graphs of Functions*

It is often useful to express the functional relationship between a dependent variable y and an independent variable x in *graphical* form. To do this, we draw two lines ('axes') at right angles to one another on a piece of graph paper, as in Figure A.1. We label the point of intersection of the two axes (the *origin* of the graph) with the figure 0. Positive values of x are measured along the horizontal axis to the right of 0; negative values of x are measured along the horizontal axis to the left of 0. Positive values of y are measured up the vertical axis above 0; negative values of y are measured down the vertical axis below 0.[4]

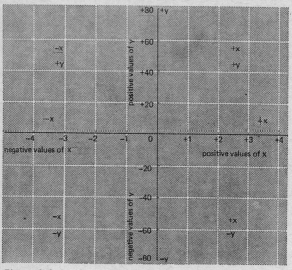

Figure A·1

(*N.B.* The *scale of measurement* which we use for one variable may be different from that which we use for the other. The units in which we measure the variables, and the scales on which they are measured, are dictated in each case largely by convenience.)

Suppose that we wish to draw a graph of the function

$$y = f(x) = x^2 - 2x - 8$$

We first make out a table in which a number of key values

4. The mathematical convention is that the independent variable (x) is measured on the horizontal axis and the dependent variable (y) on the vertical axis. The same convention is normally adopted when graphs of functions are used in the social sciences. There are some important exceptions to this, however—notably in the case of demand and supply curves in economics, where (for historical reasons) the convention is usually reversed.

are chosen for x and placed in juxtaposition with the corresponding values of y, as determined by the function:

x	-5	-4	-3	-2	-1	0	+1	+2	+3	+4	+5	+6
y	27	16	7	0	-5	-8	-9	-8	-5	0	7	16

When $x = -5$, for example, $y = (-5)^2 - 2(-5) - 8$, i.e., $25 + 10 - 8$, which = 27. When $x = 0$, $y = (0)^2 - 2(0) - 8$, i.e., $0 - 0 - 8$, which = -8. When $x = +6$, $y = (6)^2 - 2(6) - 8$, i.e., $36 - 12 - 8$, which = 16.

The *pairs* of values of x and y in the table are then plotted on a graph (Figure A.2), each pair being represented by a

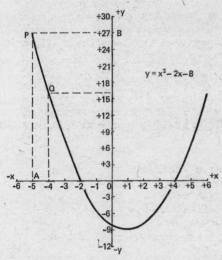

Figure A·2

single point. When $x = -5$, $y = 27$. To plot this pair of values we measure off -5 x-units along the horizontal axis to the left of 0, arriving at the point A, We then measure off 27 y-units up the vertical axis above 0, arriving at the point B. We then put a dot at the point P, which is vertically above A on the horizontal axis and level with B on the vertical axis. This point P, depending upon the way one looks at it, tells us either what the value of y will be when $x = -5$, or what the value of x will be when $y = 27$. When $x = -4$, $y = 16$, and by a similar procedure we select the point Q to represent this pair of values. Having done this for all the pairs of values of x and y in our table, we join up the dots to obtain the smooth curve in the diagram, which constitutes the graph of the function $y = x^2 - 2x - 8$ for all values of x from -5 to 6. Looking at this curve from the angle of the dependence of y upon x, we see that it traces out *the path followed by the value of y* as the value of x increases from -5 to 6.

In the social sciences, the variables concerned are usually (although not always) such that we need use only the top right-hand quarter (or *quadrant*) of the graph, since the values assumed by the variables in which we are interested are usually positive. Take, for example, the functional relationship between the demand for apples and the price of apples described in the previous section, viz.

$$y = f(x) = 40 - 3x$$

If we work out the values of y associated with different positive and negative values of x (in the same way as we have just done for the function $y = x^2 - 2x - 8$), and plot the pairs of values on a graph, we will get the straight line in Figure A.3, which, as will be seen, runs through three quadrants of the graph. In the top left-hand quadrant, however, we come face to face with a negative price, and in the bottom right-hand quadrant with a negative demand; and while it is true that plausible economic meanings could be ascribed to such phenomena, it is unlikely that they would ever be very important in the real world. Thus in this case—and in most other cases in the social sciences —the top right-hand quadrant is the only relevant one.

10. *The Slope of a Function and its Relation to 'Marginal' Quantities*

(*a*) LINEAR FUNCTIONS

A *linear function* is a function which when graphed comes out as a straight line, like the function $y = 40 - 3x$ which

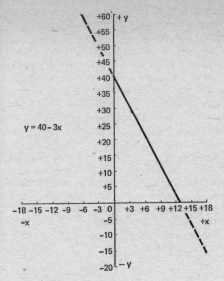

Figure A·3

we have graphed above in Figure A.3, or like the function $y = 10 + 5x$ which we now graph overleaf in Figure A.4. In the case of each of these two equations, it should be noted, the number immediately to the right of the ' $=$ ' sign represents the value of y when $x = 0$. When the function is graphed, therefore, this number is given by the point at which the line cuts the y-axis. And in the case of each equation, it should also be noted, the number by which x is multiplied (-3 in the case of the first and 5 in the case of the second) is given by the *slope* of the line which represents the function on the graph. This latter point may require some explanation.

If we are told that the *slope* (or gradient) of a road is 1 in 4, or 1:4, or 1/4, there are two possible interpretations of this piece of information. It may mean that the road rises vertically by a distance of 1 foot (or yard) for every distance of 4 feet (or yards) *measured along the road*. In other words, in terms of the accompanying diagram (which represents a cross-section through the hill up which the road travels), it may mean that the ratio of *BC to AB* is 1:4. On the other hand, it may mean that the road rises

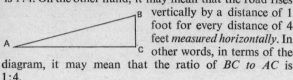

vertically by a distance of 1 foot for every distance of 4 feet *measured horizontally*. In other words, in terms of the diagram, it may mean that the ratio of *BC to AC* is 1:4.

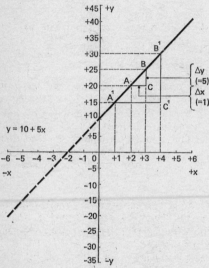

Figure A·4

It is the concept of slope implicit in the *second* of these two interpretations which is the relevant one in mathematics. In the case of a linear function $y = f(x)$, its slope is defined as the value of the ratio $\frac{\Delta y}{\Delta x}$, where Δx is some given change (whether large or small) in the value of x, and Δy is the corresponding change which takes place in the value of y when the value of x changes by Δx. In Figure A.4, for example, suppose that the value of x

increases from 2 to 3, so that $\Delta y = 5$. The *slope* of the function is then $\dfrac{\Delta y}{\Delta x} = \dfrac{BC}{AC} = \dfrac{5}{1} = 5$

It should be carefully noted that in this case we are able to say that 5 is *the* slope of the function, rather than merely the slope of the function *at a particular point*, because the slope of a straight line remains the same throughout its length. At whatever point we imagine the change in x beginning, and however large or small we make it, the ratio $\dfrac{\Delta y}{\Delta x}$ will still work out at 5. Suppose, for example, that x increases from 1 to 4, so that $\Delta x = 3$. The value of y will then increase from 15 to 30, so that $\Delta y = 15$. The slope of the function is then $\dfrac{\Delta y}{\Delta x} = \dfrac{B^1 C^1}{A^1 C^1}$ $= \dfrac{15}{3} = 5$.

In the case of the function $y = 40 - 3x$, the graph of which is redrawn in Figure A.5, the slope is calculated in the same way, but in this case, according to the convention usually adopted, it comes out as a *negative* quantity. Suppose that x increases from 6 to 9, so that $\Delta x = 3$. The value of y will then *de*crease from 22 to 13, so that $\Delta y = -9$. The slope of the function, therefore, is $\dfrac{\Delta y}{\Delta x} = \dfrac{BC}{AC} = \dfrac{-9}{3} = -3$.

It will be seen that, in the case of each of the two linear functions we have considered, the slope of the function is given by the number (on the right-hand side of the equation) by which x is multiplied.

Let us now transfer our attention to the concept of a *marginal* quantity as defined by social scientists, and in particular by economists. Suppose that we postulate the existence of a functional relationship between the total revenue received per month from the sale of a commodity (y) and the amount of the commodity produced and sold per month (x). Suppose now that the amount of the commodity produced and sold increases above its present level by an amount (Δx) which is very small in relation to this present level—an increase of 1, 2, or 3 units, say, above a present output of 5,000 units. The value of y will then change by an amount (Δy) determined by the form of the function. We define *marginal revenue* as the change in total revenue *per unit of the small change in output*— i.e., roughly, as the change in total revenue associated with the production and sale of 'one more' unit of output— and we measure it by the ratio $\frac{\Delta y}{\Delta x}$.

To take an additional example, suppose that we postulate the existence of a functional relationship between the

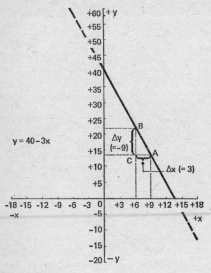

Figure A·5

total monthly output of a commodity (y) and the number of men employed to produce it (x). We then define the *marginal product of labour* as the change in total output *per unit of a small change in the number of men employed*— i.e., roughly, as the change in total output associated with the employment of 'one more' man—and we measure it by the ratio $\frac{\Delta y}{\Delta x}$.

In the case of linear functions it is very easy to work out the marginal quantity as so defined, because it is clearly equivalent to the slope of the function. The marginal quantity is the value of the ratio $\dfrac{\Delta y}{\Delta x}$ when Δx is very small.

The slope is the value of the ratio $\dfrac{\Delta y}{\Delta x}$, which as we have seen remains the same whether Δx is large or small. Thus the slope may be regarded, if we so please, as the value of $\dfrac{\Delta y}{\Delta x}$ when Δx is very small—i.e., as equivalent to the marginal quantity as defined by the economists.

(b) NON-LINEAR FUNCTIONS

A non-linear function is a function which when graphed does *not* come out as a straight line, such as the function $y = x^2 - 2x - 8$ which we have already graphed in Figure A.2, or the function $y = \tfrac{1}{3}x^2$ which we now graph in Figure A.6. In the case of a function like this we

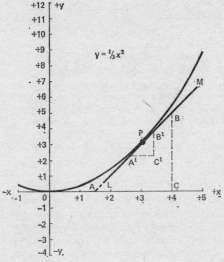

Figure A·6

cannot speak of *the* slope of the function, since its slope obviously changes continuously as the values of the variables change. All we can speak of is the slope of the function *at some particular point on the curve*—i.e., at some particular value of x. We can measure this slope by drawing a tangent to the curve at the point concerned and calculating *its* slope. Thus in the case of the function $y = \frac{1}{3}x^2$ (see Figure A.6), the slope of the function at the point where $x = 3$ will be equal to the slope of the straight line LM which is drawn tangentially to the curve at the point P (i.e., to the point on the curve vertically above 3 on the x-axis). To measure the slope of this tangent we employ the same techniques that we used when measuring the slope of our linear functions: we construct a triangle like ABC (or $A^1B^1C^1$) and measure the ratio $\frac{BC}{AC}\left(\text{or } \frac{B^1C^1}{A^1C^1}\right)$,[5] which in this case works out at 2.

Now in the case of linear functions we have seen that there is a very convenient equivalence between the marginal quantity as defined by the economists—i.e., the change in the value of y per unit of a small change in the value of x—and the slope of the function at the relevant point. It might seem, however, at any rate at first sight, that this equivalence could not possibly obtain in the case of a non-linear function like $y = \frac{1}{3}x^2$. If the value of x increases from 3 to 4, for example, the change in the value of y per unit of this change in the value of x is *not* equivalent to the slope of the function at P. It is in fact greater than this slope, as can be readily seen from Figure A.7, in which the relevant parts of Figure A.6 are 'blown up', and the curvature of the function is deliberately exaggerated. Here the change in the value of y per unit of the change from 3 to 4 in the value of x—i.e., the 'marginal' quantity—is given by the ratio $\frac{\Delta y}{\Delta x} = \frac{QR}{PR}$ = the slope of the chord PQ. But the slope of this chord is manifestly greater than the slope of the function at P. which is given by the slope of the tangent to the curve at P—i.e., by the ratio $\frac{Q^1R}{PR}$.

This apparent difficulty disappears, however, if we

5. $\frac{B^1C^1}{A^1C^1} = \frac{BC}{AC}$ by the laws of similar triangles.

remember that the definition of the marginal quantity as $\frac{\Delta y}{\Delta x}$ assumes that Δx is very small in relation to the present level of x. The increase in x which we have been postulating in our example—an increase from 3 to 4 units —is clearly *not* a very small one in this sense. Let us now

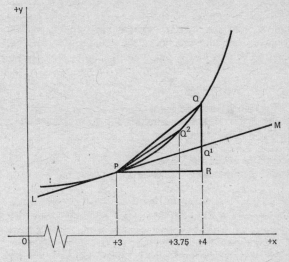

Figure A·7

postulate, then, an increase in x rather smaller than this —from 3 to 3·75 units, let us say (or from 300 to 375, if it makes things easier to imagine that we are measuring x in hundreds of units). The 'marginal' quantity will now be given by the slope of the chord PQ^2 which, although still not equal to the slope of the tangent to the curve at P, is appreciably closer to it than was the slope of the original chord PQ.

It is evident that as the magnitude of the postulated increase in x decreases, the slope of the relevant chord (measuring the marginal quantity) will approach more and more closely to the slope of the tangent to the curve at P (measuring the slope of the function at P); and that when

Δx is very small indeed—as required by the definition of the marginal quantity—the two slopes will to all intents and purposes be the same. Thus the slope of a non-linear function at any point, like that of a linear function, measures the marginal quantity as defined by the economists.

11. *The Basic Formula of the Calculus*

Suppose that a dependent variable y and an independent variable x are functionally related, the general form of the function being

$$y = ax^n$$

where a and n are parameters (i.e., numbers which do not change when the values of x and y change). We are required to work out a general formula from which we can calculate $\frac{\Delta y}{\Delta x}$ when Δx is very small indeed (in theory, *infinitely* small).

Let us suppose, first, that $n = 1$, so that

$$y = ax^1 = ax$$

We begin by assuming that the value of x changes by a finite amount Δx, and that this is associated with a change of Δy in the value of y. The same functional relationships as before will of course exist between the new quantities $(x + \Delta x)$ and $(y + \Delta y)$, so that

$$y + \Delta y = a(x + \Delta x)$$
$$= ax + a\Delta x$$

Since $y = ax$, we can cancel out these quantities from each side of the equation, obtaining

$$\Delta y = a\Delta x$$

Now we divide each side by Δx, obtaining

$$\frac{\Delta y}{\Delta x} = a$$

We now ask ourselves what (if anything) will happen to the value of each of the terms of this equation as Δx gets smaller and smaller—i.e., as it approaches zero. Nothing will happen to the value of $\frac{\Delta y}{\Delta x}$, since the function is clearly a linear one and $\frac{\Delta y}{\Delta x}$ will therefore remain constant (and equal to the slope of the function). Nor will anything happen to a, since by definition it is a parameter. Thus

$$\frac{\Delta y}{\Delta x} = a$$
(when x
approaches 0)

Now, second, let us suppose than $n = 2$, so that

$$y = ax^2$$

We assume again that the value of x changes by a finite amount Δx, and that this is associated with a change of Δy in the value of y. We thus have

$$y + \Delta y = a(x + \Delta x)^2$$
$$= a[x^2 + 2x\Delta x + (\Delta x)^2]$$
$$= ax^2 + 2ax\Delta x + a(\Delta x)^2$$

Since $y = ax^2$, we obtain

$$\Delta y = 2ax\Delta x + a(\Delta x)^2$$

Dividing each side by Δx, we obtain

$$\frac{\Delta y}{\Delta x} = 2ax + a\Delta x$$

What will happen to the value of each of the terms of this equation as Δx approaches zero? The value of $\frac{\Delta y}{\Delta x}$ will certainly not remain constant, since the function is non-linear, but this does not mean that it will approach zero. All it will do is to get closer and closer to the value of the slope of the tangent to the curve at the relevant point[6]— and this, of course, is precisely the value which we are seeking to determine. On the other side of the equation,

6. See above, pp. 223–4.

however, the term $a\Delta x$ will approach zero as Δx approaches zero, so that we are left with

$$\frac{\Delta y}{\Delta x} = 2ax$$
(when Δx
approaches 0)

Now, third, let us suppose that $n = 3$, so that

$$y = ax^3$$

After the postulated change in the values of the variables, we have

$$y + \Delta y = a(x + \Delta x)^3$$
$$= a[x^3 + 3x^2\Delta x + 3x(\Delta x)^2 + (\Delta x)^3]$$
$$= ax^3 + 3ax^2\Delta x + 3ax(\Delta x)^2 + a(\Delta x)^3$$

Cancelling out y and ax^3, we obtain

$$\Delta y = 3ax^2\Delta x + 3ax(\Delta x)^2 + a(\Delta x)^3$$

Dividing each side by Δx, we obtain

$$\frac{\Delta y}{\Delta x} = 3ax^2 + 3ax(\Delta x) + a(\Delta x)^2$$

As Δx approaches zero, the value of $\frac{\Delta y}{\Delta x}$, as before, approaches the value of the slope of the tangent to the curve at the relevant point; and the values of the two terms on the right-hand side which involve Δx will each approach zero. Thus we have

$$\frac{\Delta y}{\Delta x} = 3ax^2$$
(when Δx
approaches 0)

Collecting our three results, we find:

(1) That when $y = ax^1$, $\frac{\Delta y}{\Delta x} = a$
(when Δx
approaches 0)

(2) That when $y = ax^2$, $\dfrac{\Delta y}{\Delta x} = 2ax$

(when Δx
approaches 0)

(3) That when $y = ax^3$, $\dfrac{\Delta y}{\Delta x} = 3ax^2$

(when Δx
approaches 0)

And we would find, if we took functions involving successively higher powers of x and performed the same operation with them,

(4) That when $y = ax^4$, $\dfrac{\Delta y}{\Delta x} = 4ax^3$

(when Δx
approaches 0)

(5) That when $y = ax^5$, $\dfrac{\Delta y}{\Delta x} = 5ax^4$

(when Δx
approaches 0)

and so on. The *general* law involved now leaps to the eye: in the case of any function of the general form $y = ax^n$,

$$\frac{\Delta y}{\Delta x} = nax^{n-1}$$

(when Δx
approaches 0)

It can be proved that this result is true for *any* value of n.

12. *Dual Values for the Internal Rate of Return*

Under certain circumstances the curve relating present worth to the rate of discount may not slope downwards from left to right throughout its length, as the one in Figure 12.1 in the text does. When this happens, we may get two (or even more) values for the internal rate of return.

Take the case of a project whose characteristics are as follows:

	Beginning of 1st year	End of 1st year	End of 2nd year
Costs:	$I = 73$	$C_1 = 100$	$C_2 = 400$
Benefits:	—	$B_1 = 271$	$B_2 = 300$

In this case very heavy costs are incurred at the end of the second (and last) year of the project, so that in the second year costs exceed benefits. If the discount rate were very low—zero, say—the present worth of the project would be

$$\frac{B_1}{1+r} + \frac{B_2}{(1+r)^2} - \left(I + \frac{C_1}{1+r} + \frac{C_2}{(1+r)^2}\right)$$

$$= \frac{B_1 - C_1}{1+r} + \frac{B_2 - C_2}{(1+r)^2} - I$$

$$= \frac{271 - 100}{1+0} + \frac{300 - 400}{(1+0)^2} - 73 = -2$$

—i.e., the present worth would be negative. And if the discount rate were very high—30%, say—the present worth would also be negative:

$$\frac{\text{Present}}{\text{Worth}} = \frac{271 - 100}{1 \cdot 3} + \frac{300 - 400}{(1 \cdot 3)^2} - 73 = -0 \cdot 63$$

But at certain intermediate rates of discount the present value of the losses in the second year would fall in relative importance, and the present worth of the project would be positive, as indicated in Figure A.8. In this case, then, there are two rates of discount which would bring the project's present worth out at zero, and therefore two values for the internal rate of return—12·7% and 21·5%.

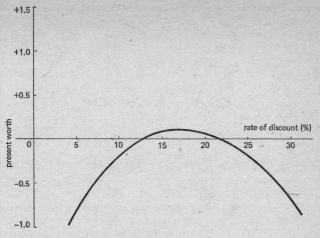

Figure A·8

13. *How the Level of the Rate of Discount May Affect the Choice Between Rival Investment Projects.*

Consider the case of two mutually-exclusive projects A and B whose characteristics are as follows:

		Beginning of 1st year	End of 1st year	End of 2nd year	End of 3rd year
Project A	Costs	$I = 50$	$C_1 = 0$	$C_2 = 0$	$C_3 = 290$
	Benefits	—	$B_1 = 0$	$B_2 = 0$	$B_3 = 400$
Project B	Costs	$I = 100$	$C_1 = 0$	$C_2 = 0$	$C_3 = 240$
	Benefits	—	$B_1 = 0$	$B_2 = 0$	$B_3 = 410$

As will be seen, each of the projects lasts three years, and it is not until the very end of this three-year period that the benefits are received and the operating costs fall due for payment. A has a lower initial capital expenditure than B (50 as compared with 100), but higher operating costs (290 as compared with 240). In other words, A is relatively labour-intensive and B is relatively capital-intensive.

Suppose now that the discount rate which we use in working out the present worths of the two projects is very low—zero, say. The present worth of A will then be

$$\text{Present Worth} = \frac{B_3}{(1 + r)^3} - \left(I + \frac{C_3}{(1 + r)^3}\right)$$

$$= \frac{B_3 - C_3}{(1 + r)^3} - I$$

$$= \frac{400 - 290}{(1 + 0)^3} - 50 = \frac{400 - 290}{1} - 50$$

$$= 60$$

The present worth of B, similarly calculated, will be

$$\text{Present Worth} = \frac{B_3 - C_3}{(1 + r)^3} - I = \frac{410 - 240}{1} - 100$$

$$= 70$$

At a discount rate of zero, then, B would appear to be preferable to A. The reason for this is that at a discount rate of zero the absolute difference between the present value of $(B_3 - C_3)$ in the case of A and the present value of $(B_3 - C_3)$ in the case of B is 60 in favour of B, and this outweighs the absolute difference between the initial capitals of 50 in favour of A.

Imagine now that the rate of discount rises above zero. As it does so, the absolute difference in favour of B between the present values of the two $(B_3 - C_3)$'s will gradually become smaller and smaller, and thus have less and less effect in offsetting the absolute difference between the initial capitals of 50 in favour of A. Sooner or later, as the rate of discount continues to rise, the present worth of A is bound to become equal to and then greater than that of B, so that A begins to appear to be preferable to B. The turning-point will occur when the discount rate has risen to the value of r in the equation

$$\frac{400 - 290}{(1 + r)^3} - 50 = \frac{410 - 240}{(1 + r)^3} - 100,$$

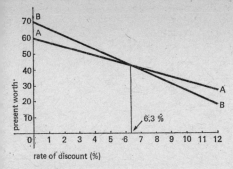

Figure A.9

which works out at $r = 0.063$, or 6·3%. Alternatively, the turning-point may be indicated by the point of intersection of the curves relating the discount rate to the present worths of the two projects (Figure A.9).

Index

Fontana Books

Fontana is at present best known (outside the field of popular fiction) for its extensive lists of books on history, philosophy, and theology.

Now, however, the list is expanding rapidly to include most main subjects. New series, sometimes extensive series, of books are being specially commissioned in most main subjects—in literature, politics, economics, education, geography, sociology, psychology, and others. At the same time, the number of paperback reprints of books already published in hardcover editions is being increased.

Further information on Fontana's present list and future plans can be obtained from:

The Non-Fiction Editor,
Fontana Books,
14 St. James's Place,
London, S.W.1.

Fontana Introduction to Modern Economics

General Editor: C. D. Harbury

Each of the six books in the series introduces the reader to a major area or aspect of modern economics. Each stands on its own, but all fit together to form an introductory course which covers most A-Level and first year university syllabuses, and those of most professional bodies.

An Introduction to Economic Behaviour C. D. Harbury

Private and Public Finance G. H. Peters

Income, Spending and the Price Level A. G. Ford

Britain and the World Economy, 1919–1970
L. J. Williams

International Trade and the Balance of Payments
H. Katrak

Mathematics for Modern Economics R. Morley

The Modern Britain Series

Readers in Sociology

This original series is designed to show how the sociologist analyses and describes the main features of a complex, modern, industrial society. Each book contains extracts by British and foreign sociologists, and each chapter has a short introduction by the editors which discusses the main issues and problems and links the extracts together. This series is of great value to all those interested in contemporary society, and not only those engaged in formal courses.

The general editors of the series are Eric Butterworth, Reader in Community Studies at York University, and David Weir, Lecturer in Sociology at the Manchester Business School.

The Sociology of Modern Britain
Edited by Eric Butterworth and David Weir
This work introduces students to the study of their own society. The chapters cover the main institutional areas of contemporary Britain—the family, community, work, class and power. The book also includes a chapter on the values implicit in British society, around which much political and social conflict is inevitably centred.

Social Problems of Modern Britain
Edited by Eric Butterworth and David Weir
This book discusses such problems as inadequate housing, environmental depreciation, poverty, immigration, racial discrimination crime, deviant behaviour and sets them in the context of the social attitudes and perspectives of the 'social problem' groups themselves.

Men and Work in Modern Britain   *Edited by* David Weir
Readings on organisational types, occupations and social status, recruitment, selection and training, career patterns, ideologies and values, deviance, leisure and unemployment, linked by critical editorial introductions.

To be published:

Social Welfare in Modern Britain
Edited by Eric Butterworth and Robert Holman

Cities in Modern Britain
Edited by David Weir and Camilla Lambert

The Fontana New Naturalist

This series is edited by John Gilmour, Sir Julian Huxley, Margaret Davies and Kenneth Mellanby. Hardcover editions, published by Collins, now include more than 50 titles. The Fontana paperback editions comprise:

Mountains and Moorlands   W. H. Pearsall

The Highlands and Islands   F. Fraser Darling and J. Morton Boyd

The Snowdonia National Park   William Condry

Britain's Structure and Scenery   L. Dudley Stamp

The World of the Soil   Sir E. John Russell

Climate and the British Scene   Gordon Manley

Pesticides and Pollution   Kenneth Mellanby

The Sea Shore   C. M. Yonge

The Trout   W. E. Frost and M. E. Brown

The Life of the Robin   David Lack

**The Open Sea: Its Natural History
Part One: The World of Plankton**
Sir Alister Hardy

A Natural History of Man in Britain   H. J. Fleure and M. Davies

The Peak District   K. C. Edwards

Wild Flowers   Gilmour & Walters

Dartmoor   L. A. Harvey and D. St Leger-Gordon

Insect Natural History   A. D. Imms

Life in Lakes and Rivers   Macan and Worthington

Figuring Out Society

Ronald Meek was born in Wellington, New Zealand in 1917 and educated at Hutt Valley High School and at the Victoria University of Wellington, from which he gained an Ll.M. in 1939 and an M.A. in 1946. In 1949 he gained a Ph.D. from Cambridge University, and from 1948 to 1959 held the post of Lecturer in Political Economy at the University of Glasgow. From 1960 to 1963 he was Senior Lecturer in Political Economy at that University, and since 1963 has been Tyler Professor of Economics at the University of Leicester. His publications include *Studies in the Labour Theory of Value* (1958), *The Economics of Physiocracy* (1962), *Economics and Ideology* (1967) and *Turgot on Progress, Sociology and Economics* (1973). Professor Meek has also been the editor of several books on the history of economic thought, and is the author of a guide to hill-walking in the Isle of Arran.